# Gold and Silver Needlepoint

# Gold and Silver Needlepoint

*Maggie Lane*

*Charles Scribner's Sons*
*New York*

**Library of Congress Cataloging in Publication Data**

Lane, Maggie.
  Gold and silver needlepoint.

  Bibliography: p.
  1. Canvas embroidery—Patterns.  2. Decoration and
ornament—East Asia.  I. Title.
TT778.C3L284 1983      746.44′2041      82-42670
ISBN 0-684-17850-8

1 3 5 7 9 11 13 15 17 19   Q/C   20 18 16 14 12 10 8 6 4 2

Printed in the United States of America.

*This book is*
*dedicated with love*
*to the memory of my father,*
*Robert John McCandliss, M.D.*

# Acknowledgments

To all those who helped make this book possible I express my thanks.

To Louise de Paoli and Richard Read for working three of the designs—To Jean Mailey, Curator, Textile Study Room at the Metropolitan Museum of Art, New York City, for her guidance and help in finding rare books and swatches of ancient textiles in the collection of treasures she guards—To Sondra M. Castille, Senior Restorer in Far Eastern Art at the Metropolitan Museum of Art, New York City, for giving me a glimpse into a rarified realm—the restoration of Oriental scrolls—To Robert Kaufmann, Librarian; Margaret Luchars, Library Technician; and to Sheila Smith and Jacqueline Rea, Keepers of the Picture Collection in the library at the Cooper-Hewitt Museum, New York City, for their courtesy, interest, and, above all, patience, whenever I visited them to search through their books and pictures—To Lans Christensen for taking the beautiful photographs for the book—To Margot Rosenmund of Margot Galleries for responding with such alacrity and efficiency whenever I needed more material with which to stitch the designs I worked for the book—And to Myles Lane, my dear husband, for putting up with a wide variety of inconveniences while I focused all my attention on needlepoint—To you, my friends, without whose help I could not have pulled things together to complete this book, my gratitude.

# Contents

# Foreword

When Howard Carter, the discoverer of Tutankhamen's tomb in Egypt, broke through the wall of the first chamber of the long-sought structure, he was asked by those standing nearby if there was anything to be seen. "Yes," he replied, "wonderful things." As you explore the charted pages of this latest volume of Maggie Lane's exquisite needlepoint designs, you too will see "wonderful things."

There is an almost irresistible temptation to write at length about the beauty and artistry of Mrs. Lane's designs. This urge is readily suppressed, however, by contemplating them; they speak most eloquently and graphically (the pun is intended) for themselves. The shimmering panels, hangings, and handbags presented here speak volumes about the creative resources of this artist.

Maggie Lane is also practical in her approach to needlepoint. She sees her designs through the eye of a tapestry needle. This does not mean in any way that her vision is narrow, limited, or distorted. On the contrary, the view is wide and searching. She continually looks for and explores subject matter that is completely appropriate for the limitations and possibilities of the needlepoint medium. That the completed work—be it a rug, a pillow, a hanging, or a handbag—is always aesthetically satisfying is testimony to the accuracy of her keen and discerning eye.

Beyond this achievement is further practicality. As the intention of Mrs. Lane as an artist and writer is to furnish the needleworker with complete material to duplicate the sample pieces, the graphs are as meticulously executed as the photographed projects. Mrs. Lane knows that an inaccurate map will lead the needlepoint traveler to an arrival at an unknown destination. To make certain there are no unrewarding side trips, the chartwork is carefully and laboriously plotted. That the tedium involved in producing such fine work does not show is simply more of the Maggie Lane approach: her desire is to send the avid needlepointer rushing to canvas, needle, and thread. "Great art conceals art" is a statement that embraces both the finished product and the graph that leads the way.

The wonder of this entire book is that not only are needleworkers able to see these "wonderful things," but unlike those excavators of the Egyptian tomb, they are able to do more than see the objects placed in protective surroundings, such as a museum; they may duplicate them for a lifetime of pleasure and, the designs being of a durable and classic style, pass them along to future generations.

Probably more than in any other form of needlework it can be said of working from a graph that every stitch counts. It is these counted stitches, of course, that bring the finished piece to perfection. We all have seen needlepoint pieces worked on a painted canvas with a barely recognizable subject matter. That problem is never encountered in a Maggie Lane design.

Aside from the simple, perfect beauty of her works, Mrs. Lane's significant achievement in the development of a modular system of needlepoint designs makes a journey on the charted path endlessly interesting. While the designs are complex—made up of several elements—they are never complicated. Many of these designs-within-designs work up very quickly and inspire the worker to proceed with more fervor to "see what happens." The graph shows the *way,* but the stitched motif is a pleasant rest stop along the trip to completion.

The use of this modular system is a further treasure to be mined by the avid and inventive needlepointer. With little effort it may be adapted for use in other projects. And if you own Mrs. Lane's four previous books of needlepoint designs, you might add further prayers for immortality: the possibilities for combinations and adaptations stretch into infinity.

I had aimed for brevity in these opening comments and have succeeded only moderately. There are several reasons for my decision to be brief:

1. When one writes that Maggie Lane's designs are simply beautiful the subject has been thoroughly covered.

2. The work, as noted before, speaks with more richness than I.

3. I feel that this foreword will be (and should be) largely unread, the reason being that a wise stitcher will turn quickly to the designs, select one to begin on, and hurriedly assemble the supplies with which to make it. That is what I plan to do.

While writing this foreword I have sought for a word or phrase to characterize the full body of Maggie Lane's works. "There must be a word," I thought; "they are so splendid." Splendid, yes. A fast paging through my dictionary let me discover that the designs—all of them and most particularly those in this book—are shining, brilliant, illustrious, and excellent. Only one semantic step remained for me to arrive at *my* appellation—Maggie Lane's Splendors of the Orient. A thrilling experience awaits you.

Charles Blackburn
Costume designer and author

# Gold and Silver Needlepoint

# Introduction

I have named this book *Gold and Silver Needlepoint* simply because I used metallic threads—either gold or silver, and in some cases both—to enhance at least one part of every design presented in the following pages.

The idea of using metal threads along with natural fibers in the making of fabrics is not a new one. In the distant past weavers began to use gold thread in conjunction with silk to create sumptuous materials in which the metal's special gleam and color gave a note of glamor to the cloth. More often than not, the metallic thread in those rich old textiles and tapestries appeared in some kind of satin or twill weave, or was laid in long flat stitches so that the brilliance of the gold remained undimmed.

In the hangings and panels I stitched for this book I did not try to duplicate those ancient damasks and brocades woven of such precious stuffs. It would have been an impertinence, because my materials—cotton and man-made metal-like filaments of mylar or nylon, stitched on fairly coarse needlepoint canvas—were too gross for such a feat. I sought instead just a breath of grandeur, and only the faintest hint of shimmer.

In my designs, gold and silver are used in a variety of ways—as an outline around a fan-shaped picture, as a glint in a repeat pattern, or as a simulated gold-leaf background. The most ambitious use of gold is, of course, the last, where it is meant to suggest the backgrounds of old Japanese screens.

There, I was surprised and pleased to discover, a sense of depth is achieved. Metallic thread, when added to cotton floss and used together with it in the needle for gold-leaf backgrounds, acts as a reflector. This seems to illuminate the space around and behind the robes and animals so that all objects worked in cotton floss alone seem to be floating in a sea of golden light.

Working large plain areas has always seemed to me to be a tedious business. Therefore, in most of the designs I have presented in my books I have tried to be kind to you, my reader, and myself, by giving both of us very few projects where the background has not been worked in a pattern.

All the "leaf" backgrounds shown in this book are worked in squares or rectangles. I must say that I have thoroughly enjoyed covering the background in this way. It is delightful to be able to pick up my canvas at daybreak and say to myself, for instance: "Today I think I will fill in the square of leaf behind the dark horse's ears."

In all the designs in this book I used D.M.C. six-strand cotton embroidery floss. In every canvas I also used gold or silver threads—alone or mixed with the floss—for backgrounds or in repeat patterns. In a few places I used Au Ver à Soie's silk floss—alone or mixed with the metallic filaments—only because that company produces so many subtle shades and colors that are simply not available in the more prosaic range offered by D.M.C. However, *nowhere* in this book—dedicated to the glories of gold and silver—have I used wool, for wool is fuzzy. And I could not bring myself to place it next to the sleek, smooth, shiny metallic filaments.

This does not mean, however, that these designs could not or should not be made entirely in wool. Any graph in this book may be worked in any kind of yarn or thread you choose to use. Here, I want to add—and *stress* the point—that the color schemes I have used are not absolute. You do not have to follow them. You are free to change any or all colors in whatever design you decide to make.

This collection of projects is for *you*. Your decision must be the final one when it comes to making something you want to carry in your hand or hang on your wall.

# Stitches

Many years ago, when I wrote my first book on needlepoint, I gathered together and put into it all I then knew about stitching. After it was published I did not stop exploring the subject. I learned more than a few new stitches, but I wrote only a few more books. Thus, *Needlepoint by Design,* the first of the set, might be called the primer in a "course" in needlepoint. The second book, *More Needlepoint by Design,* might, therefore, be called the text for freshmen; the third book, *Chinese Rugs Designed for Needlepoint,* the syllabus for sophomores; and the fourth book, *Rugs and Wall Hangings,* projects for juniors.

Here, now, is a resume of the entire course—with the oppulent addition of gold and silver—presented as a summary for seniors.

Many of you have been following the "course" since the first book appeared. Some of you, however, may be newcomers, unfamiliar with the material already covered. So for the newcomers I shall pause to review important points and facts you may have missed but need to know.

If needlepoint is a subject absolutely foreign to you, I think you should consider making a small sampler before you decide to tackle a bigger or more complicated project. I will give you a sensible reason for taking this step: you can find out whether or not you enjoy needlepoint. If you discover that you hate making stitches on canvas, throw your sampler away. If, however, doing needlepoint pleases you, keep on stitching.

Learn the basketweave stitch first (a diagram for it appears on page 142) since it is the most important stitch to master. It is worked in diagonal rows on the canvas. A stitch is formed when the yarn comes up and goes down diagonally over the crossing of a horizontal and a vertical canvas thread. On the back of the canvas, the thread then passes under two parallel horizontal or vertical threads before coming up to make another diagonal stitch over the crossing of two canvas threads. Its construction—the short diagonal stitch on the front of the canvas, countered by the longer horizontal or vertical part of the stitch hidden on the back of the canvas—does not distort the canvas and pull it out of shape to any great degree. It is, therefore, the best small, flat stitch to use for rugs, pillows, panels, wall hangings, and so on.

You must also learn the continental stitch. It is usually worked in horizontal rows on the canvas but can also be worked vertically. It is the *only* stitch to use on mono canvas when working a single row of stitches, or when stitching an outline. However, *never* use the continental stitch for background work or in more than a single row at a time. Its construction—a short diagonal stitch on the front of the canvas, which looks exactly like the basketweave stitch, followed by a long diagonal passage of thread at the back of the canvas in the same direction as the stitch on the surface—exerts a strong diagonal pull on the canvas and distorts it terribly, often beyond redemption.

A sampler is also useful in helping you to decide how many threads you must use—when working any stitch—in order to cover the canvas to your satisfaction. Everyone works with a slightly different tension. An easy tension is better than a taut one. After you have made a stitch with the needle, pull the thread trailing from the needle only to the point where the thread just barely begins to resist your pull. A finished stitch does not need to be yanked up tight. Tying a firm knot requires a hard pull. A needlepoint stitch does not, because it will not undo itself. If you have ever tried to rip out any areas of finished work you will understand what I mean.

A sampler also serves as a trial arena where you can experiment with new stitches. You can also work colors and tones next to each other on the sampler to decide if they please you.

When working on your sampler, and later, when you stitch the "serious" piece of needlepoint you plan to make, be sure that you do not allow your thread to twist or loop. Roll your needle a bit after every stitch. You will soon discover how to do this. An untwisted thread makes for smoother stitches.

# Canvas

When you are ready to tear yourself away from your sampler and get on with a real project, there are a few preliminary steps you must take.

First, select the graph you want to use, or, if you like, design a graph of your own.

In this book as well as in the others I have written, the thread count or box-stitch count of each graph is given as part of the information you will need when you key your canvas to that particular graph. The "number" of the canvas used to make the original piece of needlepoint—the sample that has been photographed for the book—is also given. For example, when the information given states that the number of the canvas used is 12, or #12, that means there are 12 canvas threads to the running inch on the canvas used to make the sample.

The size of the finished piece is also given, along with the outside measurements of the piece of canvas needed for the project. This outside measurement allows for a border of empty canvas three inches wide all around the work area.

Your next step is to buy a piece of ecru canvas of the appropriate size. I suggest ecru canvas rather than white canvas because sometimes canvas threads peek through between finished needlepoint stitches, and glimpses of ecru are less startling than glimpses of white.

If you want to make your project smaller than the original sample, select a piece of canvas with a finer mesh, that is, with more threads to the running inch. If you want to make your project larger than the original sample, select a canvas with a coarser mesh, one with fewer threads to the running inch.

Canvas is available woven in a wide variety of thread counts, all the way from #7, with 7 threads to the running inch (which means that you will work 7 stitches to the running inch), to #58, with 58 threads to the running inch. The #58 canvas is really a fine silk gauze. Some people work designs on it for dollhouse decorations, such as pillows, rugs, and wall hangings.

To figure out how large a finished piece of needlepoint will be if you use a canvas with a larger or smaller number of threads to the inch than that given in the instructions, follow this simple rule: take the *graph* thread count from top to bottom and from side to side, and divide each figure by the *number* of the canvas you have selected.

If the graph thread count is given as 120 x 240, and the canvas you have selected is #12 (with 12 threads to the running inch), divide 12 into 120, and 12 into 240. The result will be 10 and 20, which means that the finished project if worked on #12 canvas would measure 10″ x 20″.

Suppose you want your finished piece to be larger than the size just given. Let's see how large it would be if worked on #10 canvas. Divide 10 into 120 and 10 into 240. The result: 12″x 24″.

If you want to use #7 canvas, the finished piece would measure approximately 17″ x 34″.

If you want to use #18 canvas, the finished size would be a small 7″ x 14″.

Once you have decided what number of canvas you want to use, and have bought a piece of it large enough for the project, you should bind it to keep your needlepoint threads from snagging on its raw edges and to keep the canvas from raveling. You can either make a narrow hem along each edge of the canvas or you can bind it with masking tape that is about 1½″ wide. One brand of masking tape sticks to the canvas for a long time while another does not, and I have almost given up trying to remember which brand adheres and which doesn't. Instead, I use another kind of tape, made by 3M, which *does* stick to the canvas for a long time. It is a paper surgical tape called Micropore, comes in several widths, and is available in white or flesh color. Try it if you have been having bad luck with masking tape.

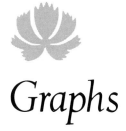

# Graphs

All of the graphs in this book, as well as all those in my earlier books, represent designs in which every stitch has been completed. In other words, each graph is a mechanical drawing of a piece of finished needlepoint.

When they first look at a needlepoint graph, many people do not understand its meaning or purpose. They think that the gray grid lines on the graph represent the threads of the canvas, and that the small white squares on the graph represent holes in the canvas. *This is not the case!*

Right now I want you to open the book to the section devoted to the graphed designs. Look carefully at any one of the graphs. You will see that the design is drawn with *lines that always follow the grid lines on the graph* and in so doing *outline areas* that have symbols marked in them. These symbols identify colors or tonal values and should tell you something—that each of these small squares on the graph represents a bit of color, or a certain tonal value, or a dot of yarn, or, perhaps, but yes, you've got it—*a stitch!*

It is really unfortunate that paper covered by row upon row of tiny ovals instead of tiny squares is not available. If only such a type of graph paper were available you would easily make the connection, for then you would surely see each oval as a stitch.

Let us try another way to understand a needlepoint graph. If you have a piece of finished needlepoint in the house, go get it. Take a good look at it. Now, imagine that you are also holding a piece of wire screen in your other hand. Each small square hole in the screen is the size of a stitch on the piece of needlepoint. Take the imaginary screen, with its little square holes that look *exactly* like the little squares on the graph, and place the screen on top of the piece of finished needlepoint. Adjust the two so that a needlepoint stitch peeks through each small square hole in the screen. You can now see what a colored graph would look like in which every stitch would be outlined by the grid lines of fine wire that make up the screen, and these grid lines would look exactly like the fine grid lines on the graph.

*Right now,* while this new way of seeing a graph is fresh in your mind, color some part of a graph in this book. Doing this may help you grasp and hold onto a new understanding of a needlepoint graph. Each small square on the graph represents a finished stitch. I shall call these small squares on the graph *box-stitches.*

Having learned this most important lesson, take another look at the graph. Every tenth line on the graph grid is a darker, heavier line. This is true both horizontally and vertically. These heavy lines divide the graph into *blocks* of small squares or box-stitches. The blocks measure 10 box-stitches by 10 box-stitches, which means that there are 100 small squares or box-stitches in each block.

The darker, heavier lines form a larger grid on the graph. You might think of these horizontal and vertical lines as longitudinal and latitudinal lines on a map. You might also think of them as city streets that divide the city into blocks, each block containing 100 houses, each house being represented on the graph by a small square, and each of these squares also representing a stitch, so there would be 100 stitches in a block.

# Keying the Canvas to a Graph

Every graph in this book has been designed to serve as a map for a journey of adventure on needlepoint canvas. You will find your way around with ease if you key your canvas to the graph. To do this, outline the work area and then divide it into blocks to match those on the graph. For this purpose, use an *indelible marker pen*. An A.D. Marker pen in dark tan is a good choice.

Near the top and near one side of your canvas, count off the number of threads you will need for the work area. As stated before, each graph gives this information as the thread count or box-stitch count. Allow for a three-inch border of blank canvas all around the work area. When outlining the four sides of the work area, draw each of the four lines *between* two parallel threads, not along a thread.

Now draw horizontal and vertical lines, 10 threads apart, within the work area. Each of these lines also must be drawn between two parallel threads, and not along a thread. These horizontal and vertical lines are the city street lines I mentioned earlier. They divide the work area into blocks measuring 10 threads by 10 threads (or 10 stitches by 10 stitches), an outlined block in which you will work 100 finished stitches. Or, as I suggested before, you are drawing city streets outlining blocks with 100 houses on each block. Surely you can see that street lines must be marked *between* canvas threads, because no self-respecting street

**11**

has any houses (stitches) in the street. And once more: *Each box-stitch on the graph represents a stitch on the canvas.*

Make sure that each horizontal line you draw on the canvas is separated from the next horizontal line by ten threads, and that each vertical line that you draw on the canvas is also separated from the next vertical line by ten threads. Again, I want to stress the point: *Draw these horizontal and vertical lines between two parallel threads.* Be very grateful that I do not ask you to draw a line along the top of a thread. The pen nib moves along easily in the trough *between* two threads, but if you try to draw a line along the top of a thread you will see how much the pen nib wavers.

Your canvas is now keyed to the graph. Look at the graph once more with the 100 small box-stitches (houses) in each block. Look at your canvas once more where each block that you have outlined is ready to be covered with 100 stitches.

I certainly do not want to confuse you at this point, but if you think about it carefully, you will realize that every needlepoint stitch is made on top of the crossing of a horizontal and a vertical canvas thread. If you want to outline an island that will accommodate 100 stitches, you must outline an area measuring 10 threads by 10 threads. These threads cross each other—intersect each other—100 times within the square block. The trough between threads, where you draw your outlines, is like a canal that separates one square island of 100 stitches from the next square island of 100 stitches. Now, you can easily see that the small squares or box-stitches on the graph represent the crossing or intersecting of canvas threads, where you will make your stitches, and *do not* represent the holes between canvas threads.

Having keyed the canvas to the graph, you can easily read from the graph as you stitch on the canvas. The blocks on each serve as a frame of reference. If you can count to ten on the graph you can also count to ten as you stitch. In fact, if you can count to ten you are in business! And remember, needlepoint is done *one stitch at a time.*

Sometimes the darker, heavier lines on the graph (those that outline blocks) seem to become indistinct when they are surrounded by tonal symbols. You can make them easier to see if you draw over them with a well-sharpened red pencil.

# Other Supplies

You will need a few more things before you can get to work. There are needles made just for working needlepoint stitches on canvas. They have blunt ends so they won't stab you as you work. They range in size from 16, the largest, to 26, the smallest. A size 18 is recommended for #12 canvas, and 20 or 22 is suitable for #14 canvas.

A small pair of scissors with sharp points will come in handy, and it is a good idea to use a thimble when you work. Learn early to put it on before you pick up your canvas and start stitching, because if you find that you *really* like needlepoint, and begin to put in long hours at it, a thimble will protect the skin on the finger that pushes the needle through the canvas. For even though the needle you will be using is blunt, an unprotected needle-pushing finger can get pretty sore.

# Beginning the Project

Now at last you are ready to begin work. I assume that you have your needles, a small, sharp pair of scissors, a thimble that fits, a piece of bound and marked canvas, many skeins of thread in assorted delicious colors, and your hands poised in midair.

But do you know how to thread a needlepoint needle? Here's how to do it fast. Hold the pointed end of the needle in your right hand between forefinger and thumb. Take up the thread in your left hand. Fold one end over the eye of the needle and pull the thread tight. Slip the needle out of the fold in the thread. Pinch the fold of thread between the thumb and forefinger of your left hand, then squeeze it and push it through the eye of the needle. Needlepoint needles have large eyes, so this should be easy. Then pull the fold through until you have a short tail of thread about 5″ in length on one side of the needle's eye and a long tail about 30″ in length on the other side of the needle's eye.

You may wonder why I have given such detailed instructions about this seemingly minute point. I want you to be able to spend as little time as possible on the least interesting part of doing needlepoint!

And now, *at last,* to work!

Please make your first stitch somewhere near the middle of the canvas. It is always easier to grasp empty canvas in your left hand while you ply a threaded needle with your right. Work from the center outward rather than the reverse, because if you begin work at the outer edge, by the time you have reached the middle of the canvas you will be forced to grasp canvas already thick and heavy with stitches.

The graph you have chosen to follow will help you decide where you will make your first stitch. (If there is an eye in the picture I always start there.)

The first stitch, of course, will have to be somewhere in a block of 100 stitches. Let us say that on the graph the block where you will begin is the fifth one down from the top and the fourth one in from the right-hand side. Locate the corresponding block on your canvas. Once you have found it you would be wise to park a spare needle in it so you do not have to keep relocating it. Thread your working needle with the color appropriate for your first stitch.

Starting several inches to the right of your parked spare needle, and going toward the left, run your working needle under and over two or three inches of canvas threads, using long basting stitches. Pull the thread along until its tail lies captive in the running stitches you have just made. Now you are ready for the first stitch.

The first stitch will be one of 100 inside the block on the canvas, the block where you parked the spare needle. Look at the graph. If the box-stitch is the third one down from the top of the block and the fifth one in from the right, locate that spot on the block on your canvas. Count three threads down from the top of the block and five threads in from the right. Where these two threads intersect—or one crosses over the other—you must make your stitch. *A stitch always covers the intersection of two canvas threads. Do not forget that on the graph it is represented by a box-stitch.*

After you have made your first stitch, make the second. Follow the design on the graph. Work until your thread is almost used up, then cast off, pushing the needle through to the back of the canvas. Turn the canvas over and run the needle through the undersides of eight or ten stitches. Clip off the excess thread. Then take the tail you left as you began work. Thread your needle with it and run the threaded needle through the undersides of eight or ten stitches. Pull the thread along until you have anchored the beginning of the first stitch. Clip off the excess thread.

Thread your needle again and anchor this second thread's tail by running the needle through the undersides of several finished stitches. Pull the thread until only a fraction of an inch of its tail is left exposed. Then turn over the canvas so you can see it from the front. Push the needle up through the hole that will start you off properly on your next stitch.

Continue working in this manner of casting on, working, casting off, casting on, working, casting off, and so on.

If perchance you discover to your horror that you are working in the wrong block on your canvas, do not despair. There is a remedy, and it is not ripping out all that lovely work. You can simply reoutline the work area. Add a row of horizontal or vertical blocks above, below, to the right or to the left of the original outline of the work area in order to rekey your canvas to the graph. This will compensate for your error. It is one of the best reasons for leaving several inches of blank canvas around the work area.

Plate 1.
**Flying Cranes Panel**
*See pages 30–33*

Plate 2.
**Fan with Flowering Peaches Panel**
*See pages 34–39*

Plate 3.
**Silver Cloud Evening Purse**
*See pages 40–43*

Plates 4 and 5.
**Pavillion Envelope Purse**
*See pages 44–49*

Plate 6.
**Bamboo Hobbyhorse Scroll**
*See pages 50–57*

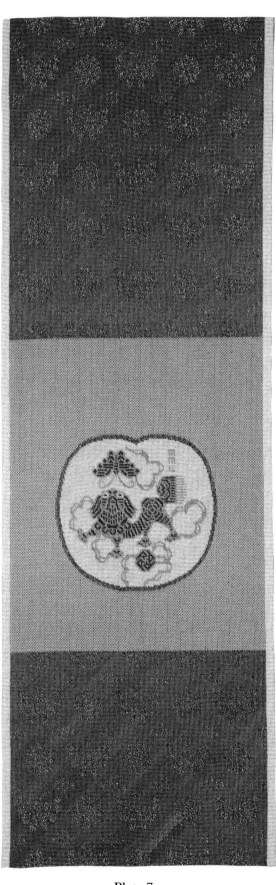

Plate 7.
**Foo Lion and Butterfly Panel**
*See pages 58–65*

Plate 8.
**Hummingbird on a Branch of Millet Scroll**
*See pages 66–73*

Plate 9.
**Swans and Lotus Flowers Scroll**
*See pages 74–85*

Plate 10.
**White Kimono Panel**
*See pages 86–95*

Plate 11.
**Three Kimonos Panel**
*See pages 96–109*

Plate 12.
**Wagon Wheels Kimono Panel by Maggie Lane**
*See pages 110–19*

Plate 13.
**Wagon Wheels Kimono Panel by Richard Read**

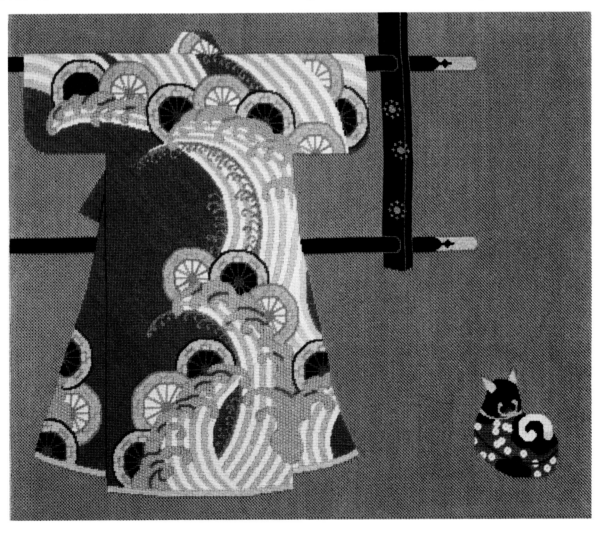

Plate 14.
**Two Horses and Groom Panel**
*See pages 120–29*

# Working with Metallic Threads

A simulated gold-leaf background is more successful, and therefore more useful in a needlepoint design, than one of silver, simply because metallic gold thread has, in itself, a medium tonal value. When lighter or darker colors are placed next to this tone, they show to good advantage. Furthermore, because of its tonal value, D.M.C. gold filament can be used in the needle with any one of the several medium-toned shades of gold-colored cotton floss that D.M.C. also makes available. A list of these follows:

| | |
|---|---|
| #422 | tan gold |
| #613 | wheat gold |
| #833 | bronze gold |
| #3013 | greenish gold |
| #3046 | muted yellow gold |

Silver, on the other hand, might just as well be thought of as being nearly white, for it can be used successfully only with the palest of grays, such as #644, #648, and #762. When one tries to achieve a pewterlike effect by using silver filaments with a darker gray floss, the result is a tweedy mixture of silver glint and sullen soot.

There is more than one brand of metallic thread suitable for use in needlepoint. D.M.C. metallic threads, namely Article 280 gold and Article 281 silver filaments, are very fine strands of synthetic material with a high metallic shine. They can be used alone when great brilliance is wanted. As mentioned earlier, the gold, when combined in the needle with a golden shade of silk or cotton floss, produces a muted cloth-of-gold effect. D.M.C. metallic thread is made in France and comes on sewing-thread spools, each containing 65 yards.

Luxofil is another brand of metallic thread one can use in needlepoint. It comes in light, medium, and dark gold, the last being of a greenish cast. It also comes in light and dark silver. The thread, or yarn, is much thicker than the D.M.C. filament. It works up well on the canvas in single, double, or multiple strands *without* the addition of cotton floss. With discretion, however, it can be combined in the needle with cotton floss. The thread also comes in several colors with a metallic shine, such as lustrous dark brown and a brilliant teal blue. Luxofil is made in Greece, and sold on rolled cardboard spools 40 meters per package.

Another brand to consider is Balger. It is made by Au Ver à Soie, the silk manufacturer, who offers 001 silver and 002 gold. The yarn has a soft shine and is a mixture of lustrous polyester and viscose wrapped around a fibrous core. It has good body and should be used alone, without the addition of cotton floss. It is *very* expensive, but works like butter! Balger is made in France and comes, 100 meters long, on a rolled cardboard spool.

A word about working with metallic threads: those that are sold already twisted around a fibrous core are easy to use. They seldom tangle or knot. But the D.M.C. metallic filaments present problems occasionally. When they do cause problems they demand enormous patience on the part of the needleworker. However, when tangles, knots, or loops appear in the threads, move the eye of the needle down the threads, all the way to the just-finished stitch. Untangle the crimps, knots, or loops, then slide the needle back to its original working place on the threads. While doing this, use the needle's eye to press out any remaining irregularities in the filaments.

If you plan to use several strands of the D.M.C. metallic filaments together in the needle—with or without the addition of cotton floss—it will help if you duplicate a contraption I made so that I could draw filaments from several spools at the same time, using only one motion.

You will need a shoe box. Near one end make two holes, one on each of the longer sides of the box. Run a chopstick or a thin dowel through four spools of filament. Insert one end of the chopstick in one hole, then slip the other end through the other hole in the box. The spools will then be suspended between the two side walls of the box. At the front end of the box make a small hole. Pull the four threads through this hole. (See Figure 1.)

Halfway along the top of the open box lay a strip of masking tape parallel to the chopstick. Press the ends of this tape to the outer sides of the box. Lay a length of double-edged tape along the top of this strip of masking tape. Use this adhesive area as a place to lay the cut ends of the filaments. They will adhere to the upper side of the double-edged tape. This will help keep each filament taut from cut end to spool. Without the addition of this refined detail, this sort of benevolent control, the cut ends of the filaments would fly around, acting as though they had a will and a life of their own.

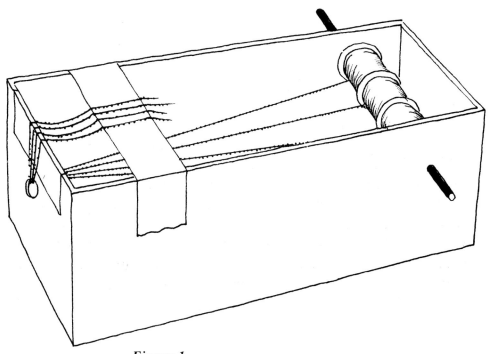

*Figure 1.*
*Shoe-box contraption for working with metallic threads*

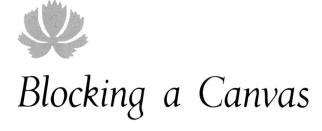

# Blocking a Canvas

A panel that will be mounted on "invisible" wooden stretchers or a piece of plywood does not need to be blocked. However, before you order a stretcher or a piece of plywood on which to mount your panel, you should tack the panel down and pull it into a rectangular shape so that you can measure it accurately. Then you can give precise measurements to the carpenter who will make the stretcher or cut the piece of plywood for you. A scroll, however, must be blocked before it is hemmed and prepared for hanging.

Lay your finished canvas face down on a large wooden surface—a big area that you do not mind piercing with tacks or staples. My solution is to use three plywood boards, each ¾″ thick and measuring 30″ x 60″. When placed side by side on the floor they provide an ideal surface for blocking needlepoint canvases. If you cover each board with muslin you will improve the surface on which you will block your work. When not in use these boards can be stored upright in a closet where they will take up little space.

*Do not wet the canvas before blocking it.* Wetting the canvas will cause it to tighten and go askew, making the blocking process very difficult, if not impossible. Instead, tack the dry canvas to the boards face down. The three-inch border of unstitched canvas that you left around your work will now perform one of its functions.

Tack or staple one end and one side of the canvas to your boards, so that the two edges of the canvas meet the two edges of the boards. I use a #10 Swingline staple gun and staples with legs ⁵⁄₁₆" long. Put the staples in close to the edge of the canvas. Then they will not get wet and rust. Do not pull the canvas too hard as you stretch it, only just enough to get out the ripples. Next, anchor the free corner of the canvas, pulling fairly hard before you finally tack it down with a few staples. These will probably have to come out later, for you will find that blocking a canvas is a process of constant correction. A screwdriver is helpful for lifting up staples that need to be removed, but I have found that a pair of small stork-billed pliers removes the staples better than any other tool.

Staple the second long side of the canvas, pulling as you go to keep it parallel to the edge of the wooden surface and the already stapled lengthwise edge of the canvas. Finally, staple the remaining loose end of the canvas to the boards. This part of the process is the most difficult, because you must see to it that all four corners of the needlepoint are square, that both sides measure the same number of inches in length, and that both ends also measure the same number of inches in width. If you see any waviness along the edges of your needlepoint, pull and restaple the canvas to eliminate the scalloped effect. I find that when I have finished blocking a canvas the staples are quite close to each other. Not much more than an inch separates one staple from the next.

At this point, dampen the canvas. Use a plastic squeeze bottle with an adjustable nozzle that will allow you to force out a fine, even mist of water. When the canvas looks as though a light dew has fallen on it, take a damp cloth and an iron set at "wool," and gently press the needlework. You can repeat the spraying and pressing as often as you like, but do not remove the canvas from the boards until it is bone-dry. Allow at least twenty-four hours after the last steaming. If the canvas remains rectangular after removal from its rigid supports, it is ready for hemming.

# Finishing a Hanging Scroll

After blocking a hanging, turn back the four sides, miter the four corners, then catch the four hems to the back of the canvas.

When mounting a hanging scroll, sew the top hem over a piece of half-round wooden dowel cut to equal the width of the panel. Lay the flat side of the dowel, 1″ in diameter, against the top back edge of the needlepoint, turn the raw canvas back over it, and roll the canvas under the piece of wood so as to cover the curved side of the dowel. Tack the rolled canvas hem to the back side of the panel. (See Figure 2. Also, take a look at an Oriental hanging scroll.) This strip of concealed half-round dowel will keep the hanging scroll from touching the wall.

At the bottom of the scroll, roll the finished hem, worked needlepoint included (the whole being the wrapping hem), around a

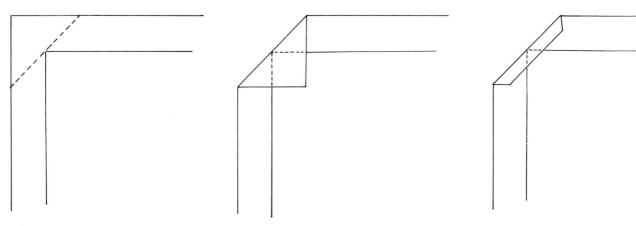

*Raw canvas*
*Fold line*

*Back of finished needlework.*
*Turn in corner and press.*

*Cut off excess canvas*
*about ½″ from fold line.*

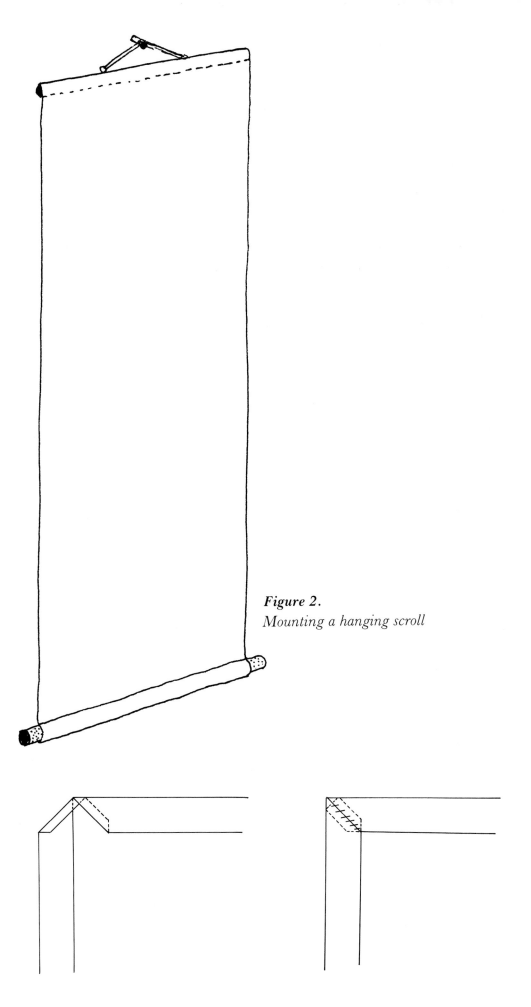

**Figure 2.**
*Mounting a hanging scroll*

*At edge of needlework, turn in one side of canvas and press.*

*Sew the two diagonal fold lines together.*

dowel 1″ in diameter, measuring 2″ longer than the width of the finished scroll. The dowel will extend an inch beyond each side of the scroll. Tack this wrapping hem, with the dowel in it, to the back of the needlepoint. When the scroll is hung, this dowel will keep the bottom of the scroll from touching the wall.

Attach a decorative cord—perhaps one crocheted of cotton floss to match the upper section of the scroll—from one "hanging strip" to the other. A knot at each end of this decorative cord will help keep it secure when you sew it to the top of the scroll. In order to hang the scroll, place this cord over a hook or nail in the wall.

It is not necessary to line a hanging scroll. In fact, I think it is inadvisable, since it only makes the scroll thicker and heavier.

# Mounting a Panel

A panel is a canvas mounted on an invisible wooden support, or stretcher. Have a carpenter make a wooden frame ¾″ in depth. He should make it with a narrow raised rim along the four outer edges on the front side of the stretcher so that the stitched part of the mounted panel touches wood only where it crosses this outer rim. If the panel is quite large, ask the carpenter to put one or two recessed supports, or struts—like railway ties—between the long sides of the stretcher. This will help to keep the stretcher from warping or going askew.

Mounting a panel is not a problem for anyone familiar with stretching primed canvas in preparation for painting a picture. For those who have never tackled such a task, however, let me suggest that you begin by marking the center of each of the four sides of the wooden stretcher. Mark the centers of the top, the bottom, and the two sides of your needlepoint panel. Place the four center marks on your panel against the four center marks on the frame. Turn the raw canvas surrounding your work back along the sides of the stretcher. Staple this raw canvas to the stretcher's sides. Start from the four center points and work toward the four corners. Work all four sides concurrently, that is, shoot in a few staples to the left of the center staple at the top of the panel and drive in a few staples to the right of the same center staple. Repeat this process on the bottom of the panel. Follow the same procedure on the two sides of the panel. From this point on, keep working from the centers toward the corners, always driving in only a few staples at a time so that you keep the tension on the needlepoint even. When you reach the four corners, fold the excess canvas so that it presents as little bulk as possible, then staple these folded corners in place.

Once this part of the mounting process has been completed, take the remaining excess canvas and fold it flat across the back of the stretcher and staple it there. Do this all the way around the back of the stretcher.

You can now remove the staples on all four sides of the panel, those used in the first step of mounting. The panel should show, at this point, smooth, taut needlepoint across its surface and bare, unstitched canvas along its four sides. The staples on the back of the stretcher are, of course, invisible when the panel is hung. If you do not like the look of bare canvas on the top, bottom, and two sides of the mounted panel, you can cover it with twill or tape or any kind of concealing material you think appropriate. Ecru canvas covering the four sides of a stretcher supporting a panel pleases me, however, so I never try to hide it.

# A Few Incidental Suggestions

Needlepoint canvas is woven with a selvage along each edge. While you are working on the canvas between these two selvages, the canvas tends to stretch a bit, but the selvages will not stretch. Before you start to work on a large piece of canvas it is wise to make snips in the selvage every two or three inches. Snip only the selvage, not the canvas proper. The purpose of doing this is to ease the tension of the selvage and allow it to stretch along with the canvas.

Some people may find the graphs in this book a little small for easy reading. In this case, have an enlarged photostat made of the graph you want to use. Then you should experience no difficulty in reading from it as you work on your canvas.

While you are in the process of making a large hanging, it is wise to press it from time to time. Use a damp cloth and a hot, but not too hot (wool setting), iron. Straighten out the area already worked. Pull it while pressing in order to rectify the slight distortion caused by the tension of your stitches. If you do this regularly, the piece will be almost rectangular when it is finished. But no matter how rectangular it seems, a piece of finished needlepoint—unless it is to be mounted as a panel on a stretcher—should be blocked before being hemmed and hung.

When working large objects in a design, it helps to outline them in the continental stitch, and then fill them in with the basketweave stitch. Even smaller areas can be managed easily in this fashion.

On #12 canvas, a skein of D.M.C. 6-ply cotton embroidery floss should work approximately 600 stitches. A strand of 6 ply is made up of 6 threads. Use 9 threads in the needle for the basketweave. Use 12 threads, or two strands of 6 ply, when working the brick stitch.

On #14 canvas, a skein of D.M.C. 6-ply cotton embroidery floss should work approximately 900 stitches. Use 6 threads, or one strand, in the needle for the basketweave. Use 9 threads, or 1½ strands, when working the brick stitch.

Use this information as a guide when buying D.M.C. 6-ply cotton embroidery floss for use in a needlepoint project.

# The
# Projects

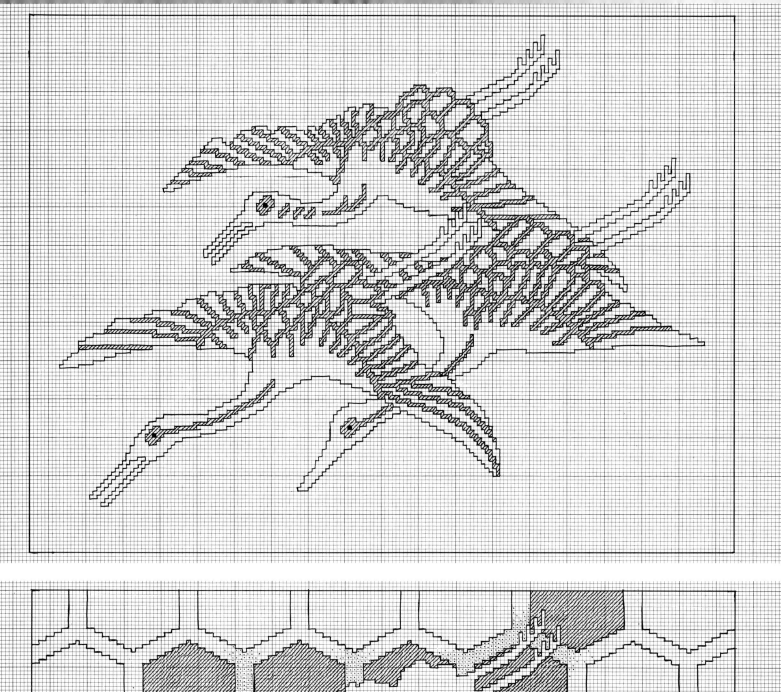
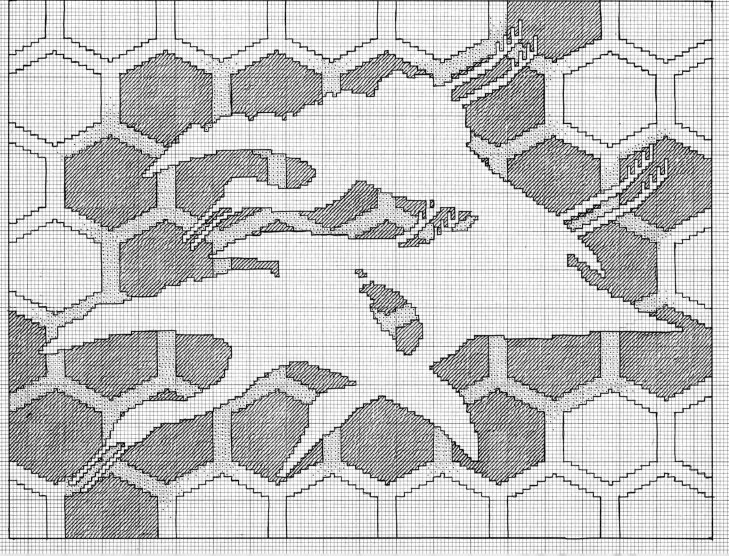

# Flying Cranes Panel

**The finished size is 11″ x 16″.**
**The original panel was worked on #12 canvas.**
**The graph box-stitch or thread count is 140 x 190.**

Buy a piece of #12 canvas measuring 17″ x 22″. Bind your canvas.

To duplicate the original panel, use the following colors:

#640 dark taupe D.M.C. 6-strand cotton embroidery floss for the pupils in the birds' eyes
#644 light taupe D.M.C. cotton for the lines in the birds
#746 off-white (yellowish) D.M.C. cotton for the birds
Luxofil dark silver mixed with #644 light taupe D.M.C. cotton for the honeycomb pattern in the background
Luxofil dark gold for the ground behind the honeycomb pattern

The entire panel is worked in the basketweave stitch. It is mounted on a panel of wood measuring 11″ x 16″ x ¾″.

The design was adapted from an old Japanese textile.

The original panel was worked by Maggie Lane.

Approximate time required for work: 45 hours.

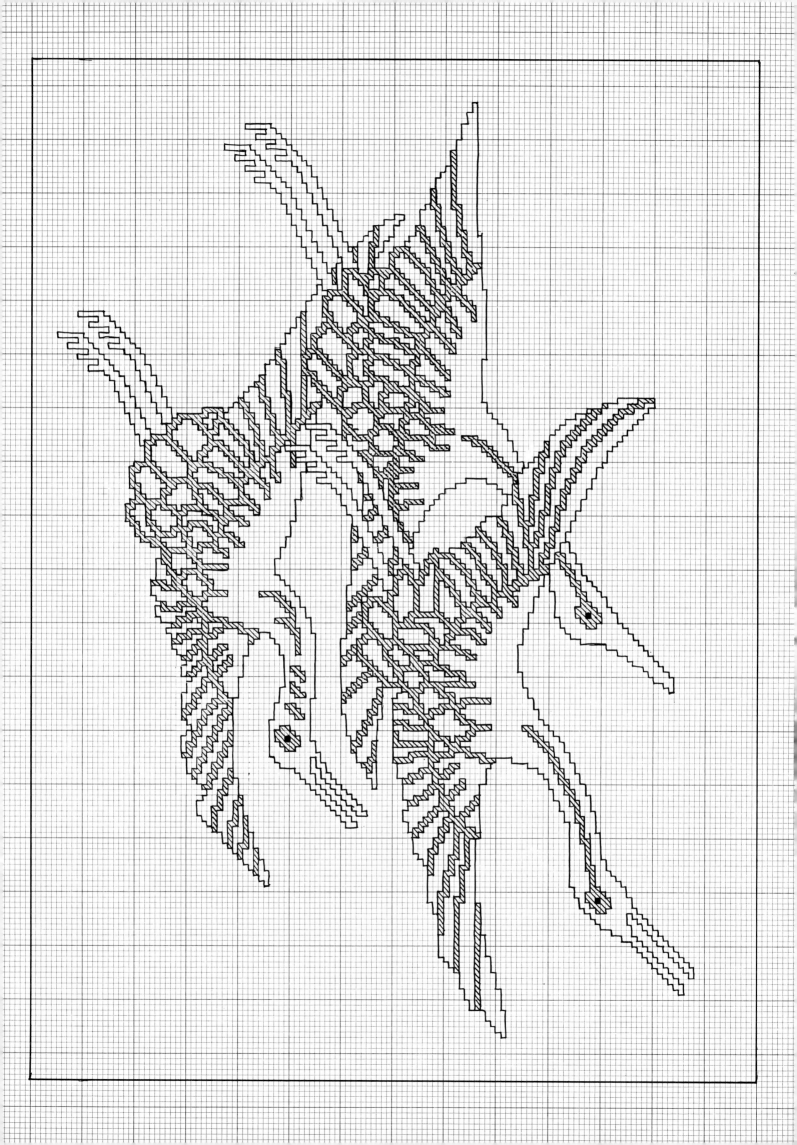

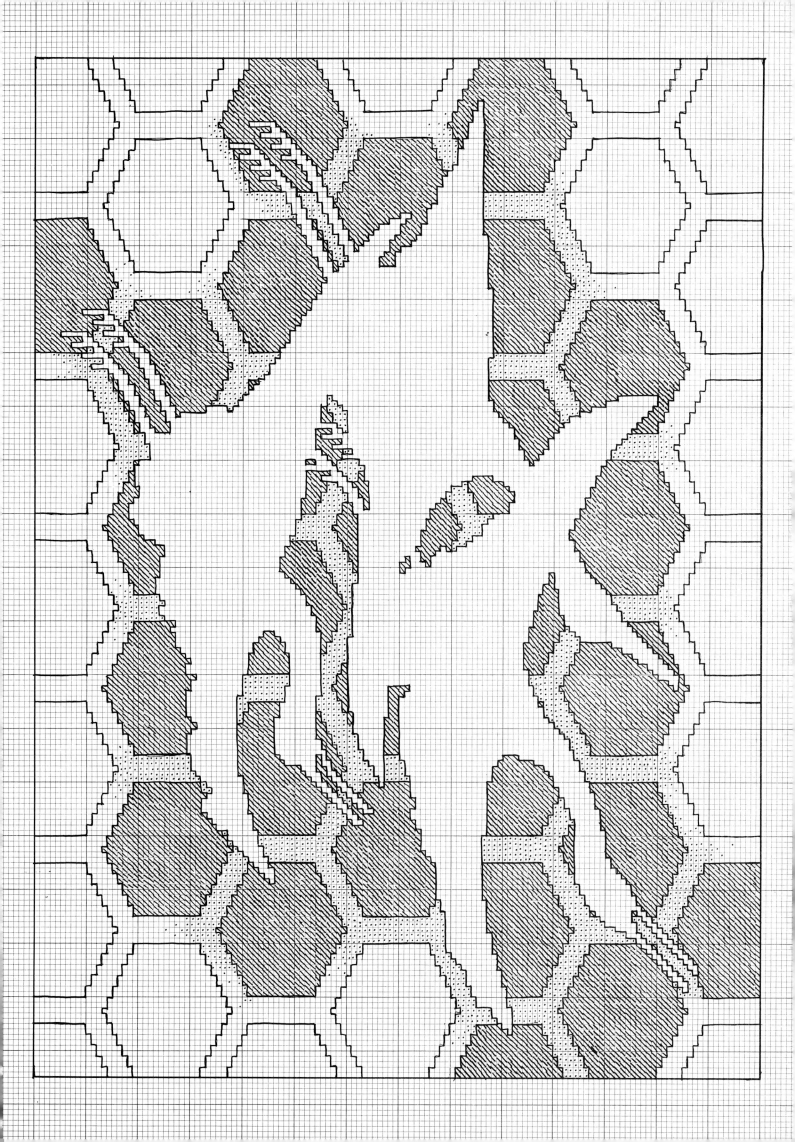

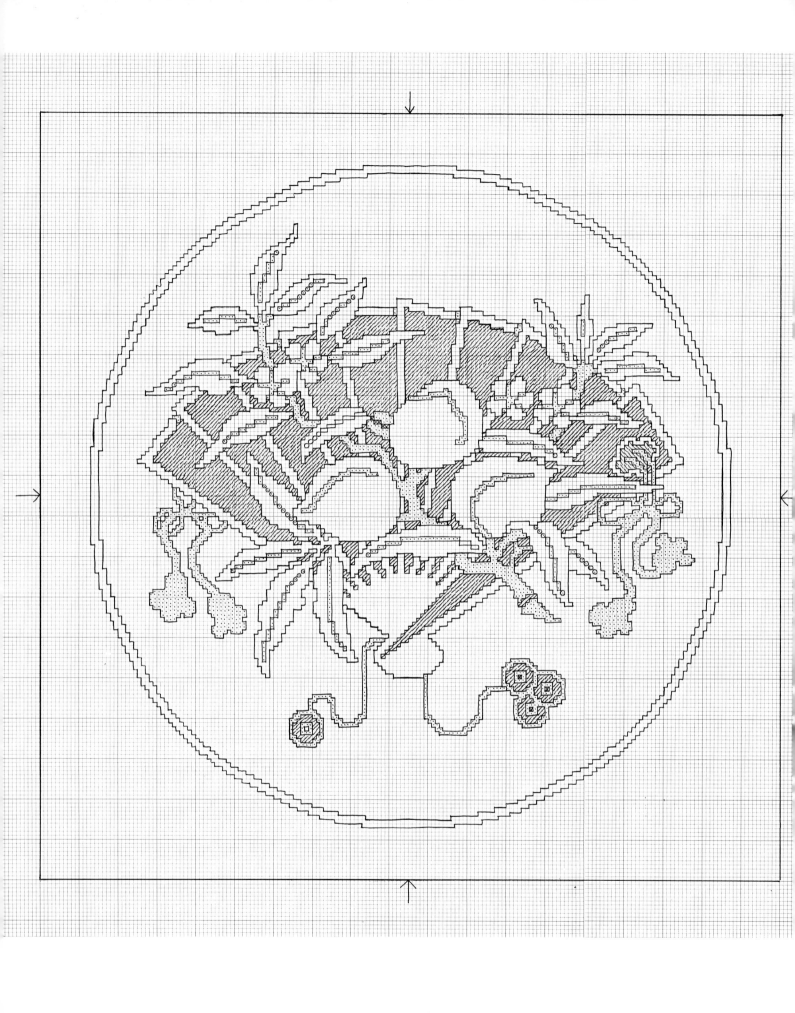

# Fan
# with Flowering Peaches Panel

**The finished size is 16″ x 16″.**
**The original panel was worked on #12 canvas.**
**The graph box-stitch or thread count is 190 x 190.**

Buy a piece of canvas measuring 22″ x 22″. Bind your canvas.

To duplicate the original panel, use the following colors:

#613 tan D.M.C. 6-strand cotton embroidery floss
#642 medium taupe D.M.C. cotton
#644 light taupe D.M.C. cotton
#645 dark gray D.M.C. cotton
#646 medium gray D.M.C. cotton
#648 light gray D.M.C. cotton

In the original panel the tones and colors are so close that I will give you some help:

1. The lines in the fruit are worked with 9 strands of #642 taupe. The fruit is worked in a Smyrna cross-stitch. The under cross is worked with 6 strands of #613 tan and 4 strands of D.M.C. Article 280 gold filament. All 10 strands are used together in the needle. The upper cross is worked with 4 strands of D.M.C. gold filament.

2. The branches are worked in #642 taupe.

3. The veins in the leaves are worked in 9 strands of #647 gray. The leaves are worked in 6 strands of #644 taupe with 4 strands of D.M.C. Article 281 silver filament. All strands are used together in the needle.

4. The flowers are worked with 6 strands of #648 light gray and 4 strands of D.M.C. Article 281 silver filament. All 10 strands are used together in the needle.

5. The outline and the base of the fan are worked in #613 tan.

6. The background of the fan is worked in #646 gray.

7. The bows, the tassels, and the ties with the cash endings are worked in #642 taupe. The cash are filled with #647 gray except for the center stitch, which is #646.

8. The background around the fan is worked in #645 gray.

9. The outline around the circle is worked in #642 taupe.

10. The background around the circle is worked in #644 light taupe. It is worked in the brick stitch. Use 12 strands of floss, i.e., double the 6 strands that cling together as you unwind the skein.

With the exception of the outer background and the fruit, the entire panel is worked in basketweave, using 9 strands of the D.M.C. 6-strand cotton embroidery floss.

The design was adapted from a detail of an antique Japanese textile.

The panel is mounted on a piece of wood measuring 16″ x 16″ x ¾″.

The original panel was worked by Maggie Lane.

Approximate time required for work: 70 hours.

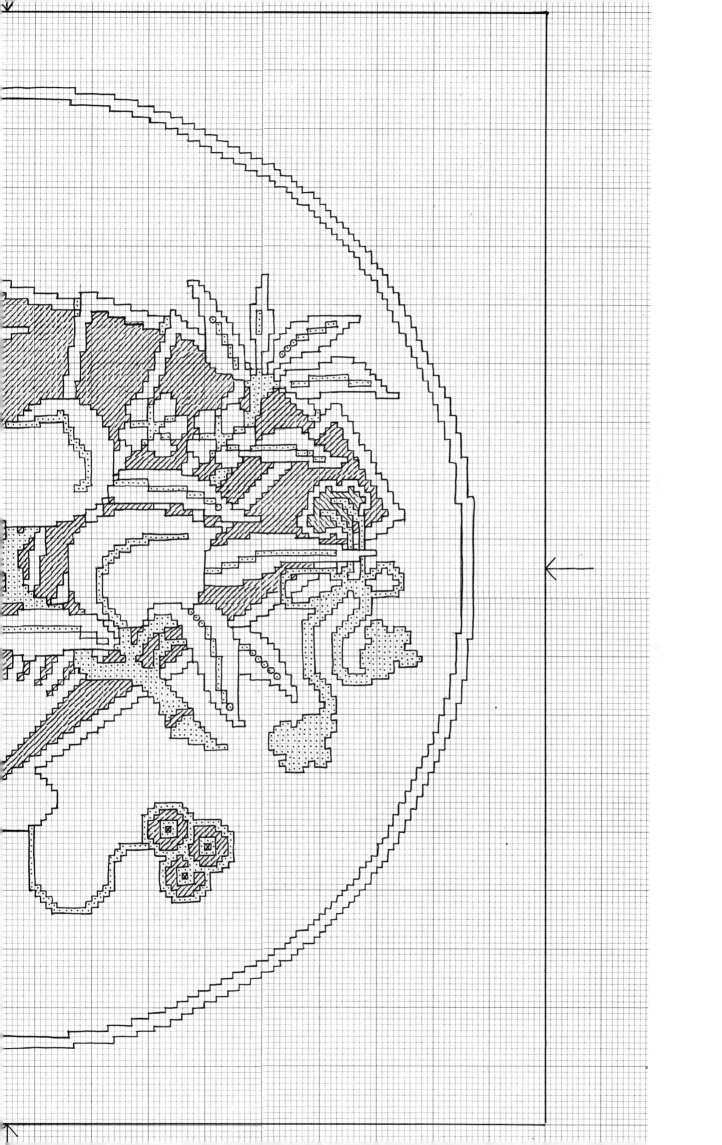

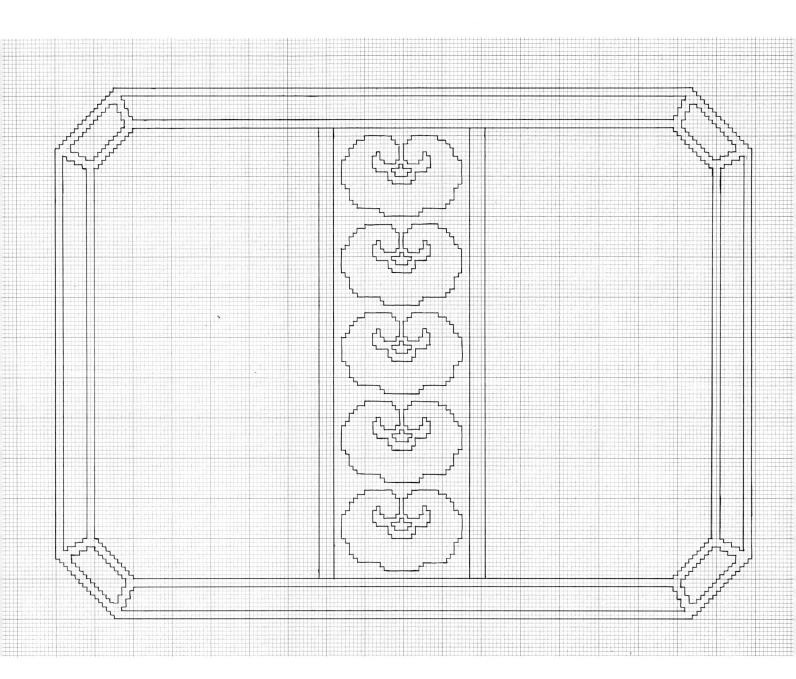

# Silver Cloud Evening Purse

**The finished size is 9¾″ wide x 7½″ high.**
**The original purse was worked on #18 canvas.**
**The graph box-stitch or thread count is 179 x 132.**

Buy 2 pieces of #18 canvas measuring 16″ x 12″, or one piece measuring 16″ x 22″, and work the two sides of the handbag on this latter one piece of canvas. Bind the canvas.

To duplicate the original purse, use the following colors:

#310 black D.M.C. 6-strand cotton embroidery floss (use 5 strands in the needle for the basketweave)

#920 red D.M.C. cotton (use 8 strands in the needle for the brick stitch)

Luxofil dark silver (use 2 strands in the needle for the basketweave)

Follow the placement of colors as shown in Plate 3.

The design was adapted from a cigarette case by Tamisier of Paris, seen opposite page 116 of *Art Deco* by Victor Arwas (*see* Bibliography). The bag was put together by Artbag Creations (*see* Suppliers). Before you start the project, write to Artbag to see how much they will charge. There may also be someone in your locality who can do the job.

The original purse was worked by Maggie Lane.

Approximate time required for work: 80 hours for the two sides.

**41**

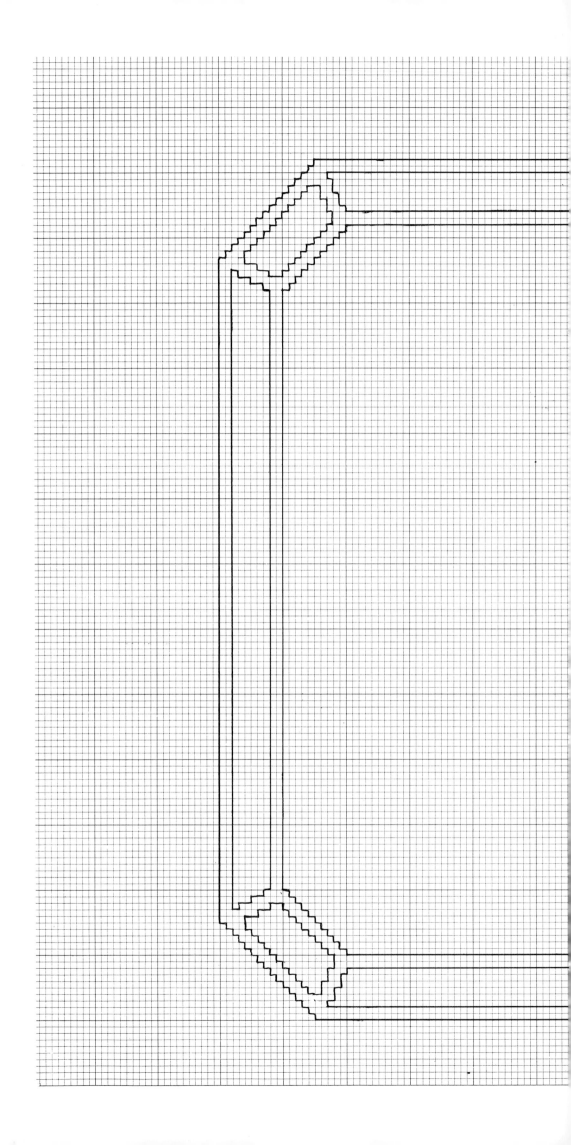

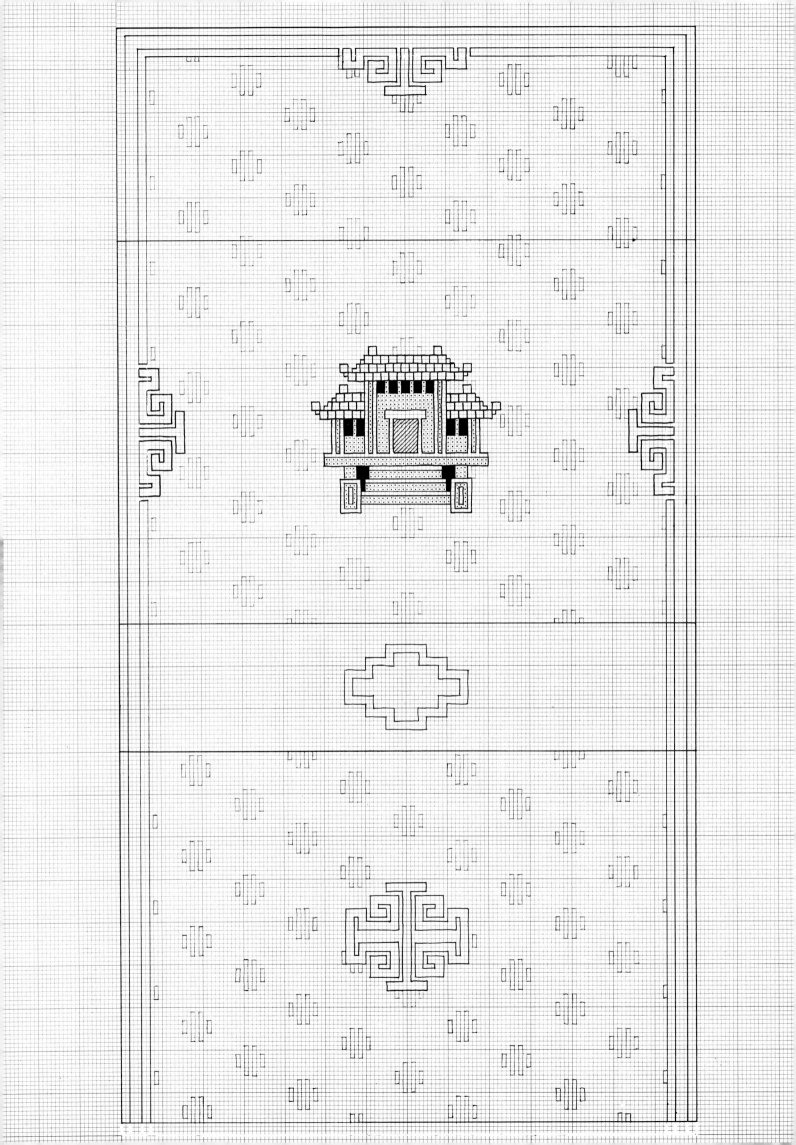

# Pavillion Envelope Purse

**The finished size is 10″ x 17¾″.**
**The original purse was worked on #14 canvas.**
**The graph box-stitch or thread count is 140 x 257.**

The size of each of the two gussets to be worked is 4″ across the top, 7½″ from top to bottom, and 2¾″ across the bottom. See the gusset diagram on page 49, which is shown actual size.

Buy a piece of #14 canvas measuring 15″ x 30″. This will be large enough to work the bag and the two gussets. Bind the canvas.

To duplicate the original envelope purse, use the following colors:

> #310 black D.M.C. 6-strand cotton embroidery floss
> #301 dark coral D.M.C. cotton
> #822 beige D.M.C. cotton
> #3712 pale celadon silk from Au Ver à Soie
> #3835 dark greenish brown silk from Au Ver à Soie
> Luxofil dark gold thread (three spools)

Follow the placement of colors as shown in Plates 4 and 5.

The roof of the pavillion is worked in staggered Smyrna cross-stitch using 3 strands of #822 beige cotton. (See page 143 for a diagram of the stitch.) The horizontal lines of the background pattern are worked in the continental stitch using #310 black cotton and #3835 dark greenish brown silk. Work one color with the

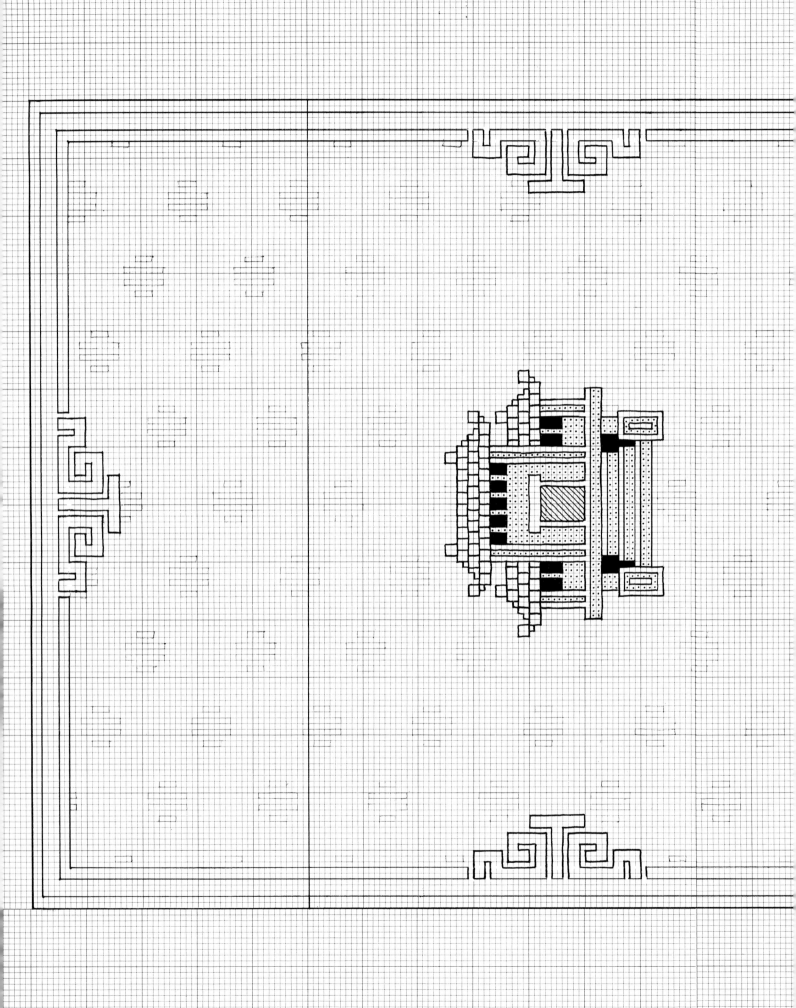

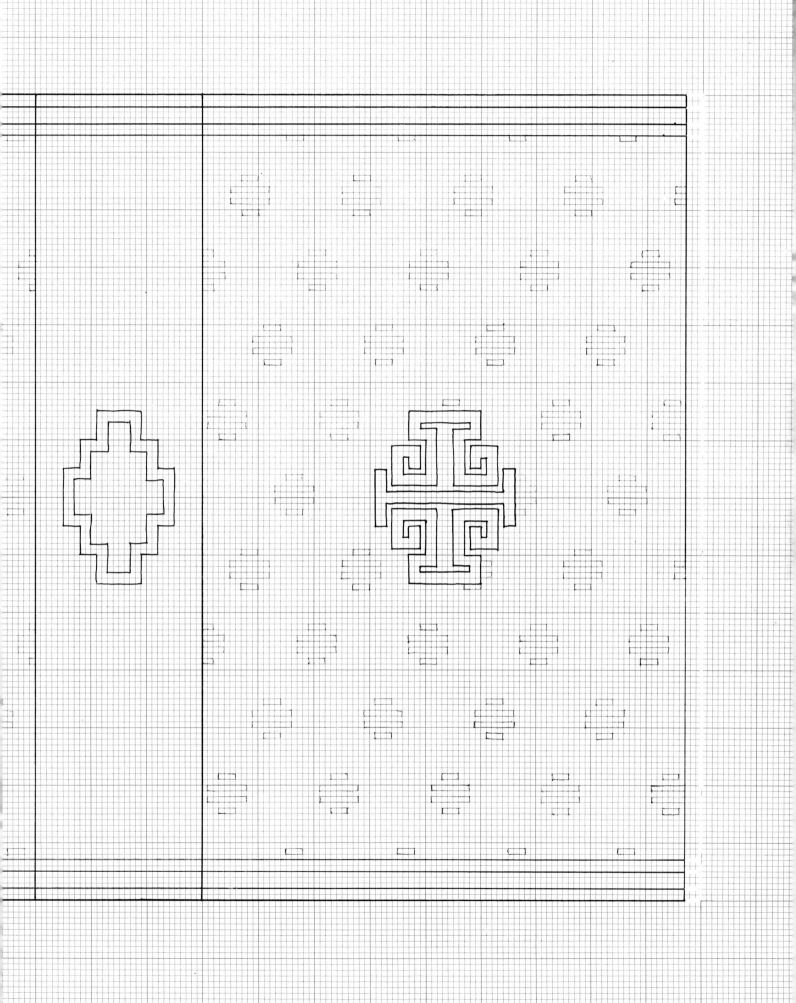

stitches slanting in one direction (///), and the other color with the stitches slanting in the opposite direction (\\\). The vertical lines in the background pattern are worked in the greenish brown silk with the addition of the Luxofil dark gold. Use 3 strands of silk and 2 strands of the dark gold together in the needle. If you want more shimmer use the metallic thread alone.

The gussets and the bottom of the bag are worked in #310 black cotton. Work your initials on the bottom of the bag and the border around them in #822 beige, and fill in the background within the small cartouche with #301 dark coral cotton.

Except for the roof of the pavillion and the background, everything else is worked in basketweave.

The purse was put together by Artbag Creations (*see* Suppliers). Write to them before you begin the project to see how much they will charge. There may also be someone in your locality who can do the job.

The original purse was worked by Louise de Paoli.

Approximate time required for work: 74 hours.

**4″**

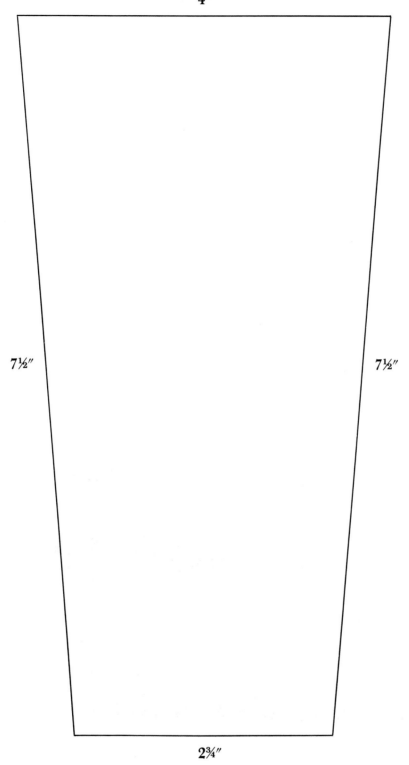

**7½″**                    **7½″**

**2¾″**

*Actual size of gusset for Pavillion Envelope Purse*

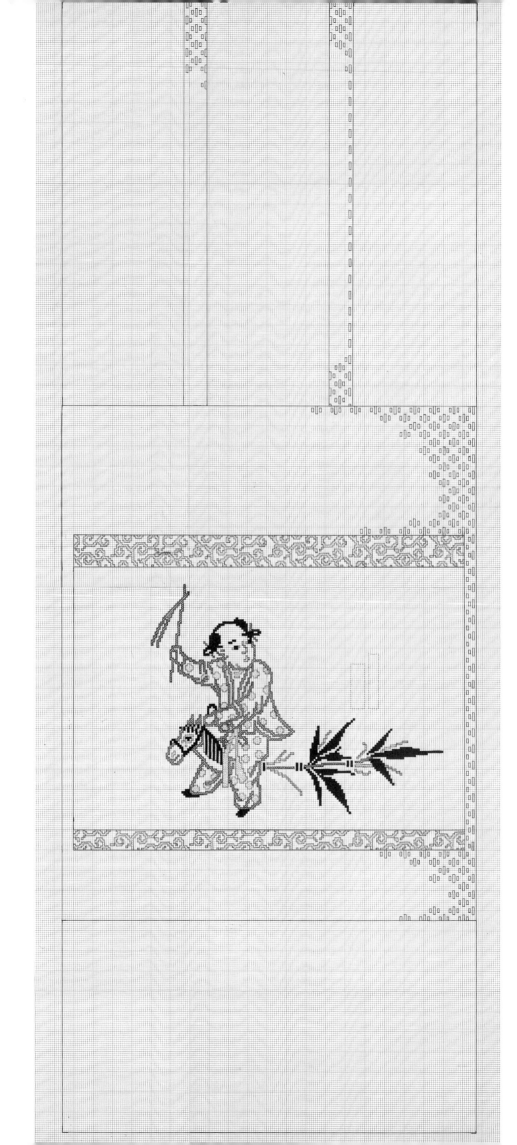

# Bamboo Hobbyhorse Scroll

**The finished size is 14½″ x 36″.**
**The original scroll was worked on #14 canvas.**
**The graph box-stitch or thread count is 213 x 560.**

There are three sections in the graph. The thread count for each section follows:

Top section, 213 x 200
Center or pictorial section, 213 x 255
Bottom section, 213 x 105

(The bottom section allows for a "wrapping hem" designed to enclose a wooden rod or dowel 1″ in diameter. This rod should be 16½″ in length so that it can extend 1″ beyond each finished edge of the panel.)

Buy a piece of #14 canvas measuring about 20″ x 40″. Bind your canvas.

To duplicate the original scroll, use the following colors for the pictorial section:

#301 rust D.M.C. 6-strand cotton embroidery floss
#336 navy D.M.C. cotton
#644 beige D.M.C. cotton
#645 medium gray D.M.C. cotton

#647 light gray D.M.C. cotton
#822 off-white D.M.C. cotton
#844 dark gray D.M.C. cotton
Luxofil dark gold

Follow the placement of colors as shown in Plate 6.

Work in the basketweave stitch, using the 6 strands of floss that cling together as you unwind the skein.

For the top and bottom sections, use #3011 olive green D.M.C. cotton. Work in the brick stitch. Use 12 strands by doubling the 6 strands you used in the basketweave stitch.

For the "hanging straps" in the top section, use #336 navy D.M.C. cotton and #822 off-white D.M.C. cotton. Work this patterned area in the basketweave stitch.

The design was adapted from a ceramic pillow at the Metropolitan Museum of Art, New York.

The scroll mounting design was adapted from a Japanese scroll. The small white repeat pattern on the dark blue background is like the Chinese character for "small," which I thought appropriate for the small boy on the hobbyhorse.

The original scroll was worked by Louise de Paoli.

Approximate time required for work: 230 hours.

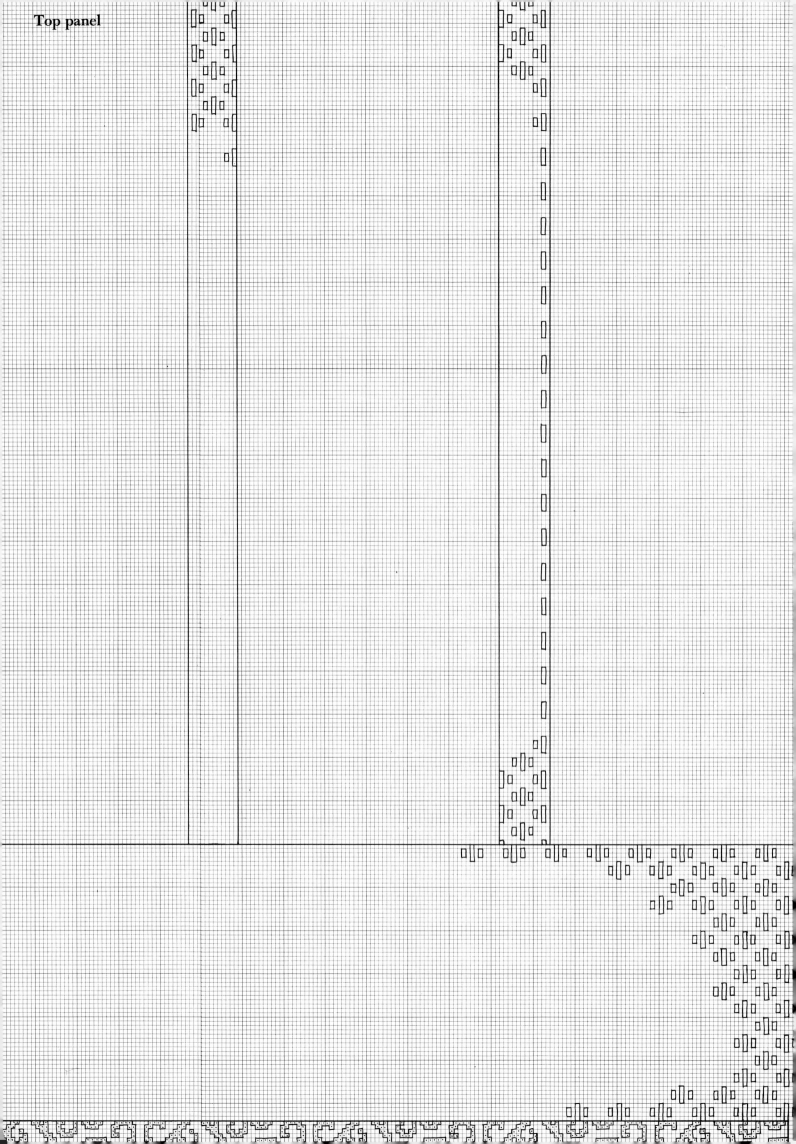

**Top panel**

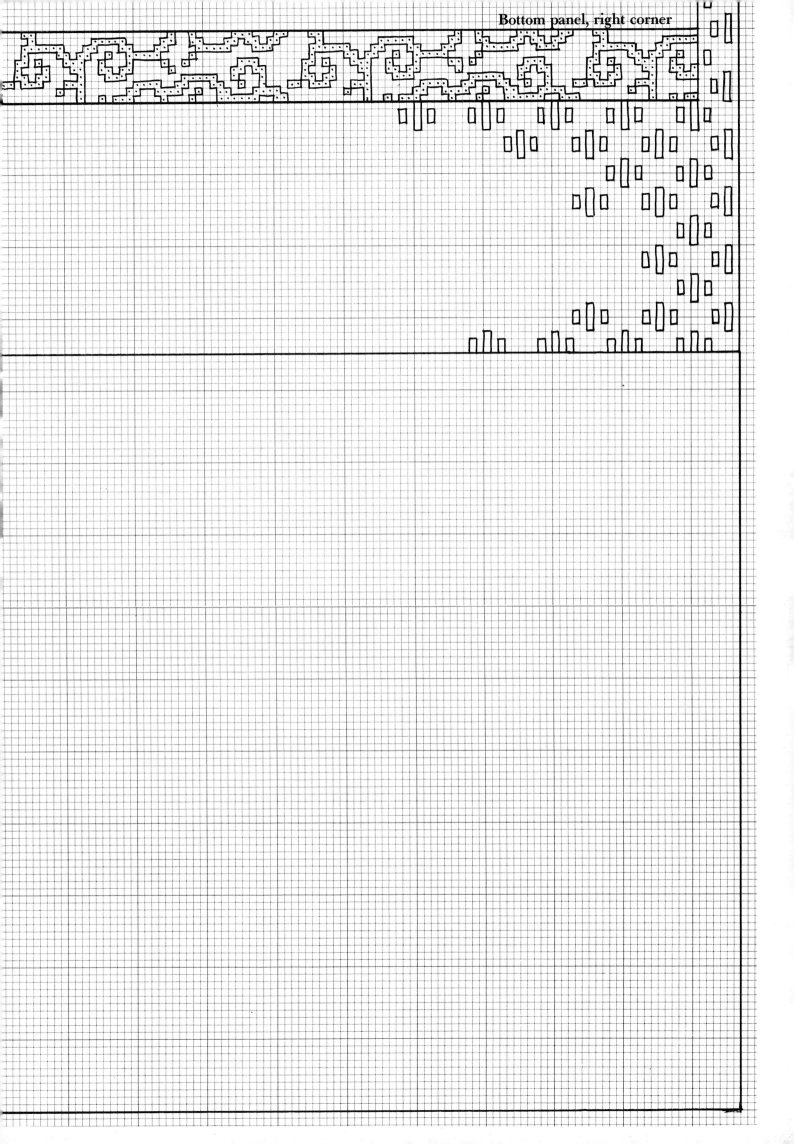

Bottom panel, right corner

# Foo Lion and Butterfly Panel

**The finished size is 15½″ x 45½″.**
**The original panel was worked on #14 canvas.**
**The graph box-stitch or thread count is 221 x 625.**

There are three sections in the graph. The thread count for each measures:

    Top section, 221 x 235
    Center or pictorial section, 221 x 235
    Bottom section, 221 x 155

Buy a piece of #14 canvas measuring 20″ x 50″. Bind your canvas.

To duplicate the original panel, use the following colors:

    #642 light greenish taupe D.M.C. 6-strand cotton embroidery floss
    #3011 dark olive drab D.M.C. cotton
    #3012 olive drab D.M.C. cotton
    #644 neutral beige D.M.C. cotton
    #436 dusky apricot D.M.C. cotton
    #543 shell pink D.M.C. cotton
    Luxofil gold, medium dark

Follow the placement of colors as shown in Plate 7.

A few helpful notes follow:

1. The Foo lion and the butterfly are worked in #642 and #3011 against a background of #644.

2. The gold border outlining the fan-shaped pictorial area is worked in three strands of Luxofil gold.

3. The dusky apricot area around the outlined pictorial area is worked in the brick stitch. All other areas are worked in basketweave.

4. The design in the top and bottom sections is worked in Luxofil gold against a background of #3012.

5. The vertical border bands along the sides of the panel, running the entire length from top to bottom, are worked in #543 shell pink.

The design is adapted from a Chinese paper cutout. It has been framed in a type of Japanese mounted-painting format.

The original panel was worked by Maggie Lane.

Approximate time required for work: 250 hours.

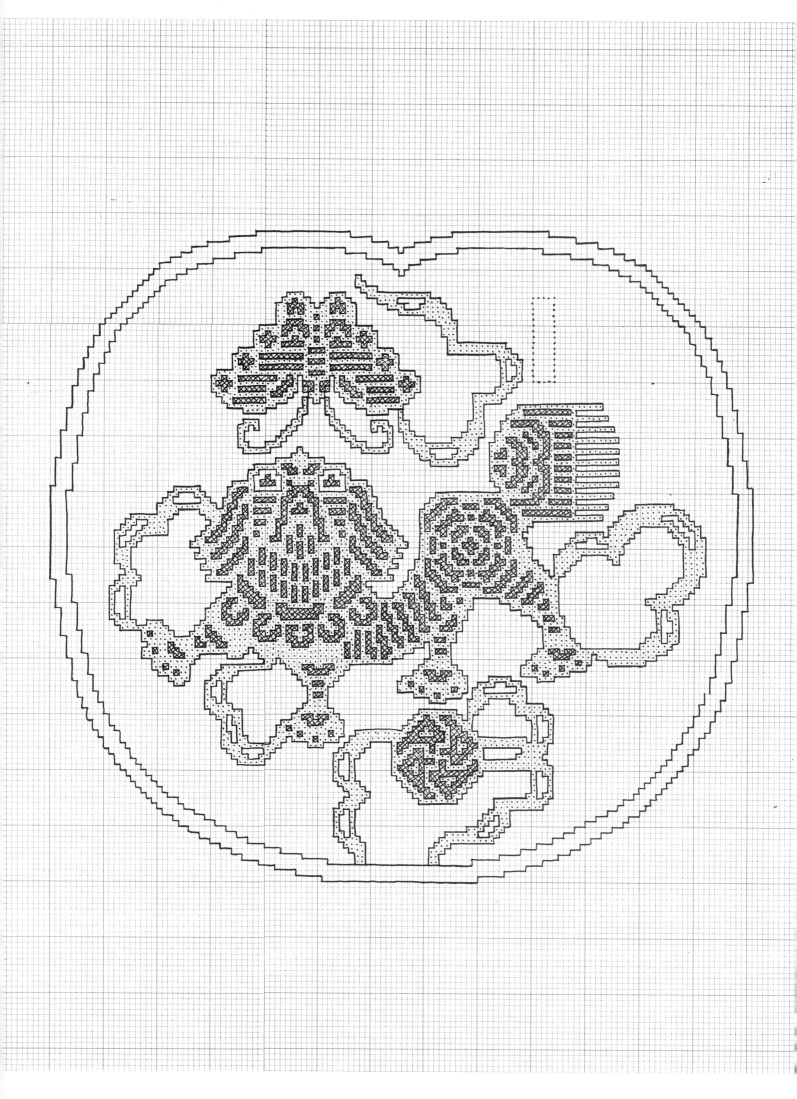

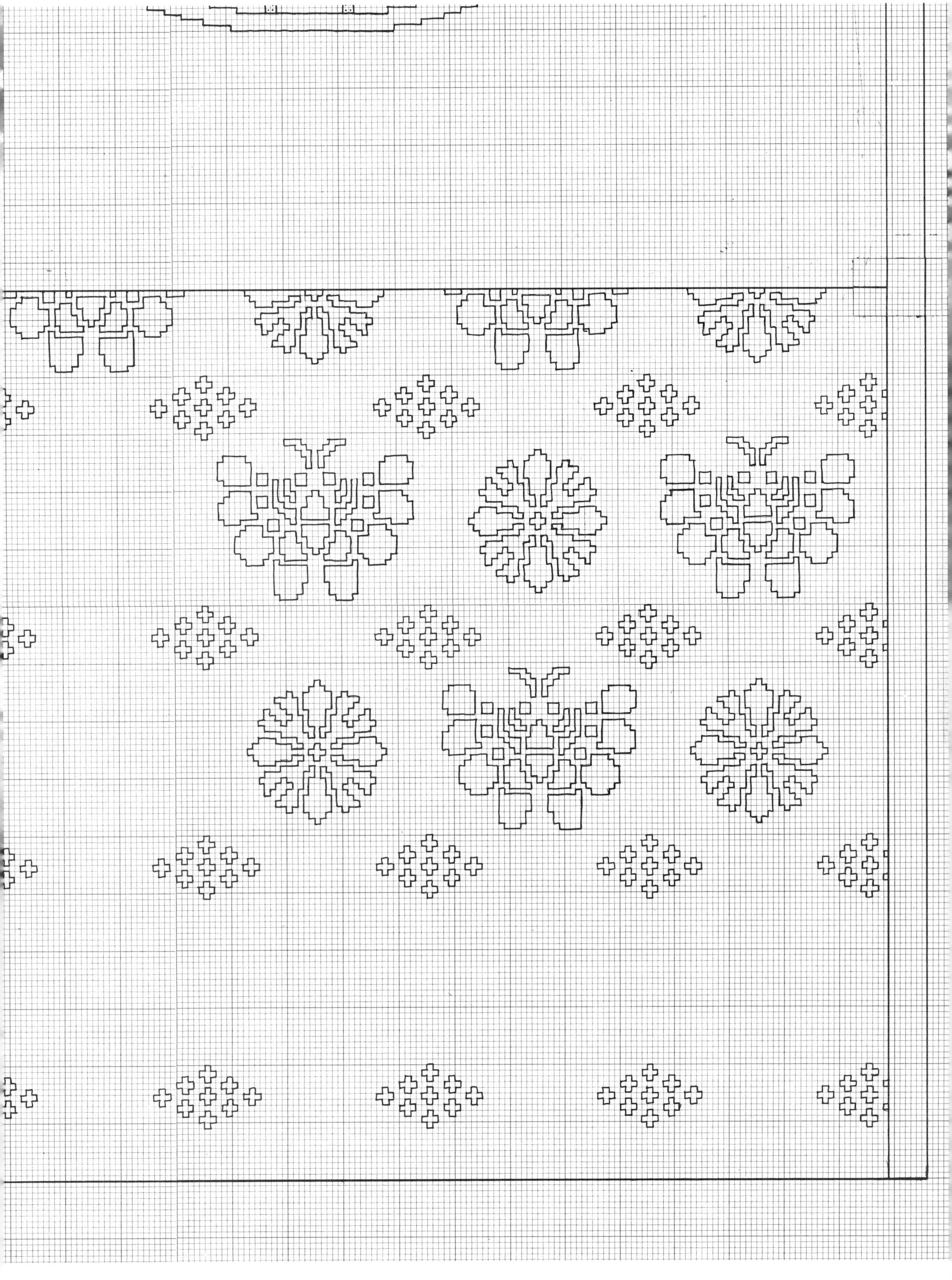

Top panel (seen lengthwise)

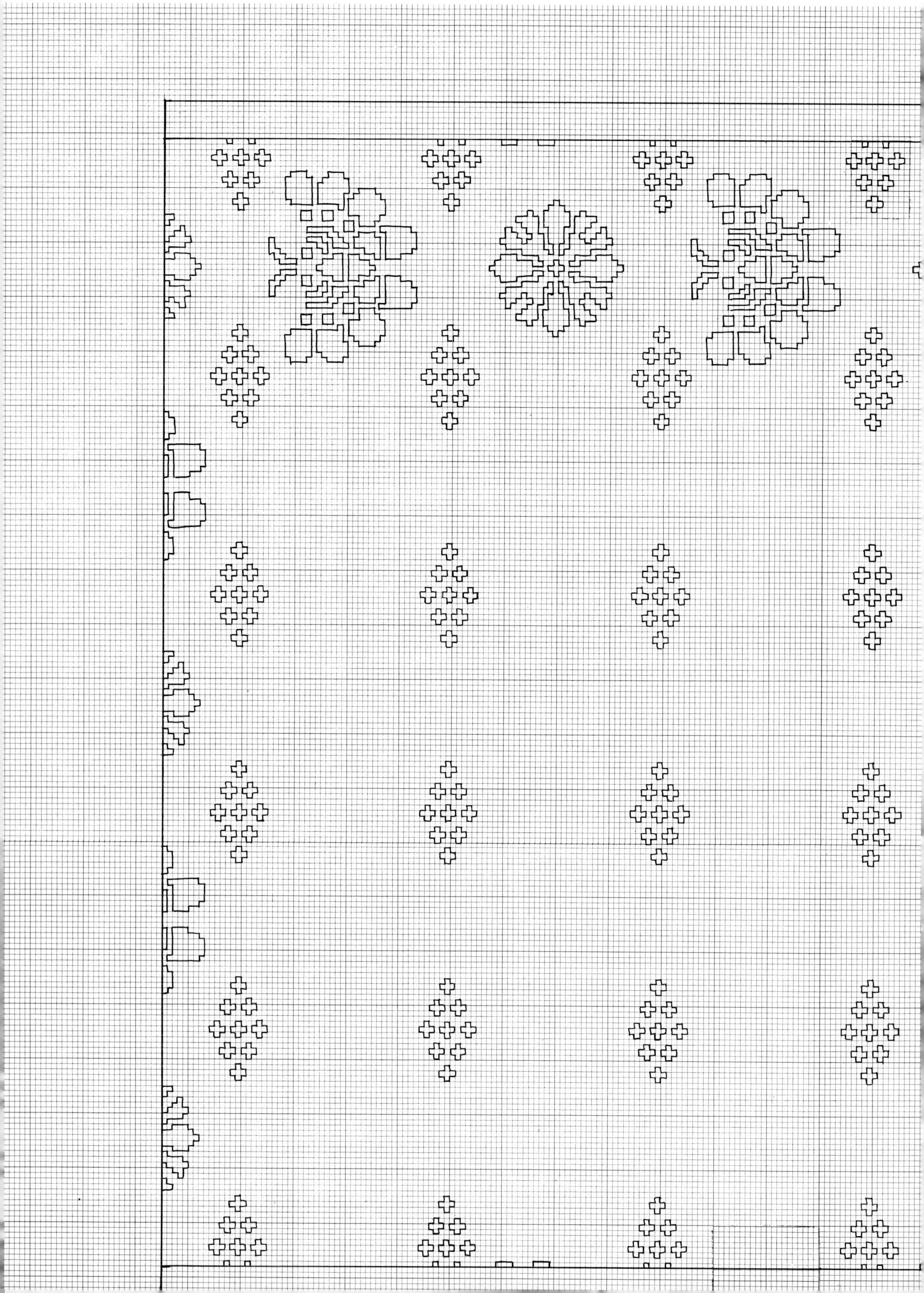

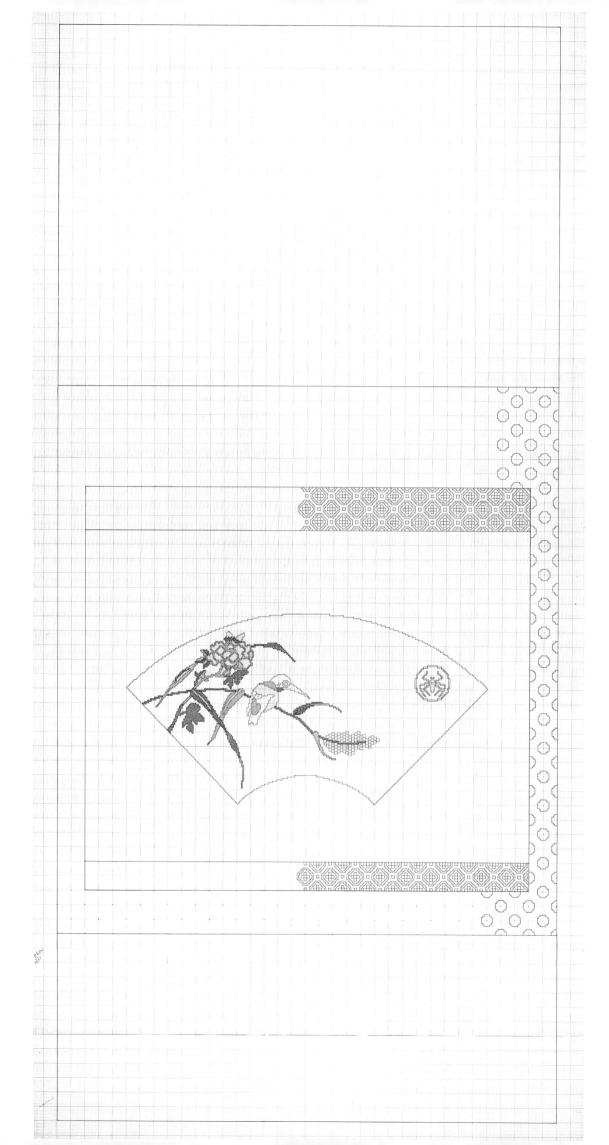

# *Hummingbird on a Branch of Millet Scroll*

**The finished size is 26″ x 54″.**
**The original scroll was worked on #14 canvas.**
**The graph box-stitch or thread count is 360 x 760.**

There are three sections in the graph. The thread count for each measures:

> Top section, 360 x 250
> Center or pictorial section, 360 x 380
> Bottom section, 360 x 130

(The bottom section allows for a "wrapping hem" designed to enclose a wooden rod or dowel 1″ in diameter. This rod should be 28″ in length so that it can extend 1″ beyond each finished edge of the panel.)

Buy a piece of #14 canvas measuring about 30″ x 60″. Bind your canvas.

To duplicate the original scroll, use the following colors for the pictorial section:

> #310 black D.M.C. cotton 6-strand cotton embroidery floss
> #420 rust D.M.C. cotton (for the spider in the circle)
> #644 beige D.M.C. cotton
> #3021 light taupe D.M.C. cotton

#3022 medium light taupe D.M.C. cotton
#3023 medium taupe D.M.C. cotton (for the background around the fan and in the bird)
#3024 dark taupe D.M.C. cotton.

Follow the placement of colors as shown in Plate 8.

The pattern directly above and below the picture is worked in the basketweave stitch using:

#644 medium beige D.M.C. cotton
#822 light beige D.M.C. cotton
#3023 dark taupe D.M.C. cotton
#3046 flaxen yellow D.M.C. cotton
D.M.C. Article 280 gold filament (for bumps)

The patterned area around the picture and its upper and lower horizontal bands are worked in 3 strands of #3046 flaxen yellow D.M.C. cotton mixed with 4 strands of D.M.C. Article 280 gold filament, all 7 strands used together in the needle for the large eyelet pattern (see page 145 for diagram of buttonhole half moons), and #413 blue gray for the background.

For the top and bottom sections use #420 rust D.M.C. cotton. The stitch used in the sample is a flat stitch, a medieval German whitework pattern (see page 144 for diagram). Use 12 strands of the cotton by doubling the 6 strands that cling together as you unwind the skein. The "hanging straps" in the top section are worked in the basketweave stitch.

The design was adapted from a Chinese album-leaf painting.

The scroll mounting design was adapted from a Japanese scroll.

The original scroll was worked by Maggie Lane.

Approximate time required for work: 450 hours.

68

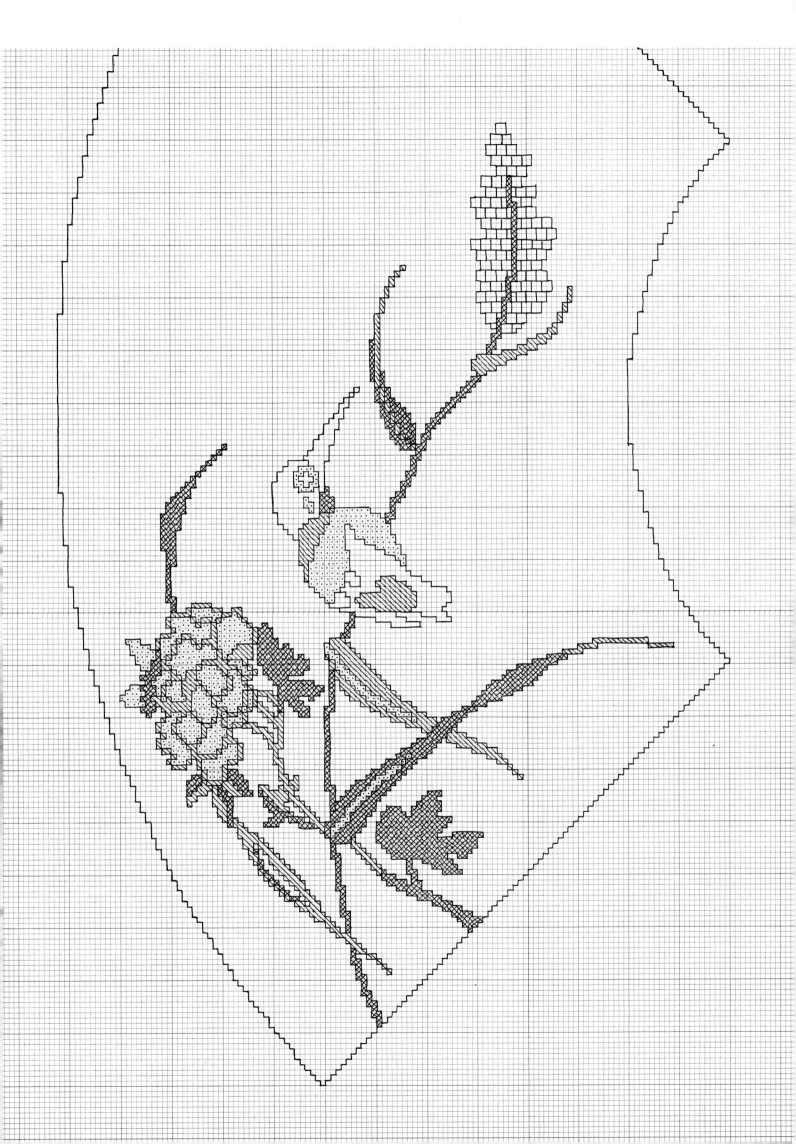

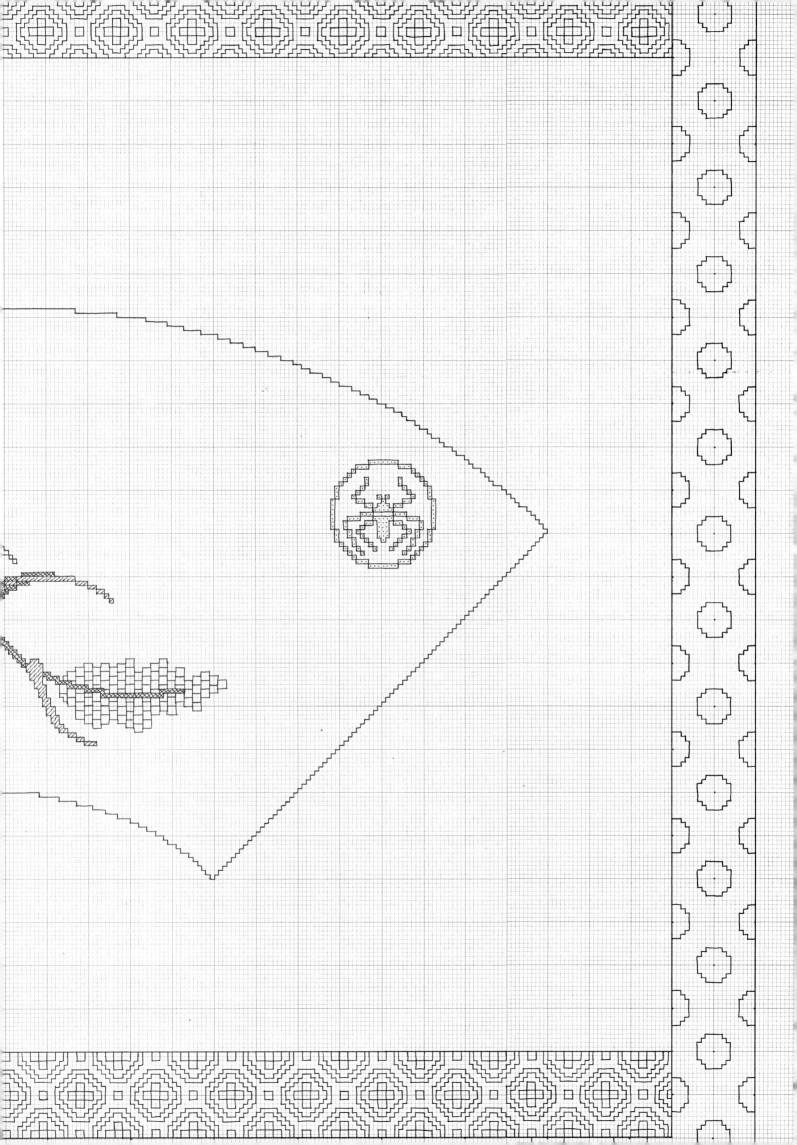

# Swans
# and Lotus Flowers Scroll

**The finished size is approximately 32″ x 63″.**
**The original scroll was worked on #12 canvas.**
**The graph box-stitch or thread count is 350 x 710.**

There are three sections in the graph. The thread count for each measures:

Top section, 350 x 237
Center or pictorial section, 350 x 333
Bottom section, 350 x 110

(The bottom section allows for a "wrapping hem" designed to enclose a wooden rod or dowel 1″ in diameter. This rod should measure 38″ in length so it can extend 1″ beyond each finished edge of the panel.)

Buy a piece of #12 canvas measuring 40″ x 84″. Bind your canvas.

The entire scroll is worked in the basketweave stitch.

To duplicate the original scroll, use the following colors for the pictorial section:

#613 tan D.M.C. 6-strand cotton embroidery floss for the swans
#822 off-white D.M.C. cotton for the swans

#3045 tan D.M.C. cotton for lines on beak, nostrils, and dark area around eye, and for stems and undersides of tan leaves

#420 ginger D.M.C. cotton for large patch on beak

#310 black D.M.C. cotton for beak

#950 pale salmon pink D.M.C. cotton in lotus flowers

#3064 dark salmon pink D.M.C. cotton in lotus flowers

#402 cantaloupe D.M.C. cotton for tiger lilies

#945 pale cantaloupe D.M.C. cotton for tiger lilies

#407 rust D.M.C. cotton for tiger lilies

#832 tan D.M.C. cotton for tiger lily stems

#2135 olive green Au Ver à Soie silk for tiger lily leaves and for outlining the three long leaves behind the tree trunk

#3872 sand Au Ver à Soie silk for veins in tan leaves (tan leaves are in #3045 tan D.M.C. cotton. See above.)

#2114 light green Au Ver à Soie silk for veins in green leaves

#2124 green Au Ver à Soie silk for green leaves

#3031 brown D.M.C. cotton for tree trunk

#3371 dark brown D.M.C. cotton for tree trunk

#611 brown D.M.C. cotton for water lines in lower right-hand corner

#610 darker brown D.M.C. cotton for background of picture

For the light-colored fretwork bands immediately above and below the picture, use #822 white D.M.C. cotton for the pattern; for the background, use 6 strands of #613 tan D.M.C. cotton and 4 strands of D.M.C. Article 280 gold filament. All 10 strands are used together in the needle.

For the carnation pattern use #644 light taupe D.M.C. cotton, #642 medium taupe D.M.C. cotton, #640 dark taupe D.M.C. cotton, #613 tan D.M.C. cotton, 6 strands, plus 4 strands of D.M.C. Article 280 gold filament. All 10 strands are used together in the needle to work the flowers.

For the top and bottom sections, use #336 dark blue D.M.C. cotton, #640 dark taupe D.M.C. cotton, 6 strands, plus 2 strands of Luxofil darkest gold (it has a greenish cast). All 8 strands are used together in the needle.

For the "hanging straps" in the top section, use #642 medium taupe D.M.C. cotton and #640 dark taupe D.M.C. cotton.

The design was adapted from a Chinese painting of the eighteenth century.

The pattern in the top and bottom sections was adapted from an old Japanese fabric in the Designer Collection in the Metropolitan Museum of Art's Textile Study Room, New York, New York.

The original scroll was worked by Maggie Lane.

Approximate time required for work: 450 hours.

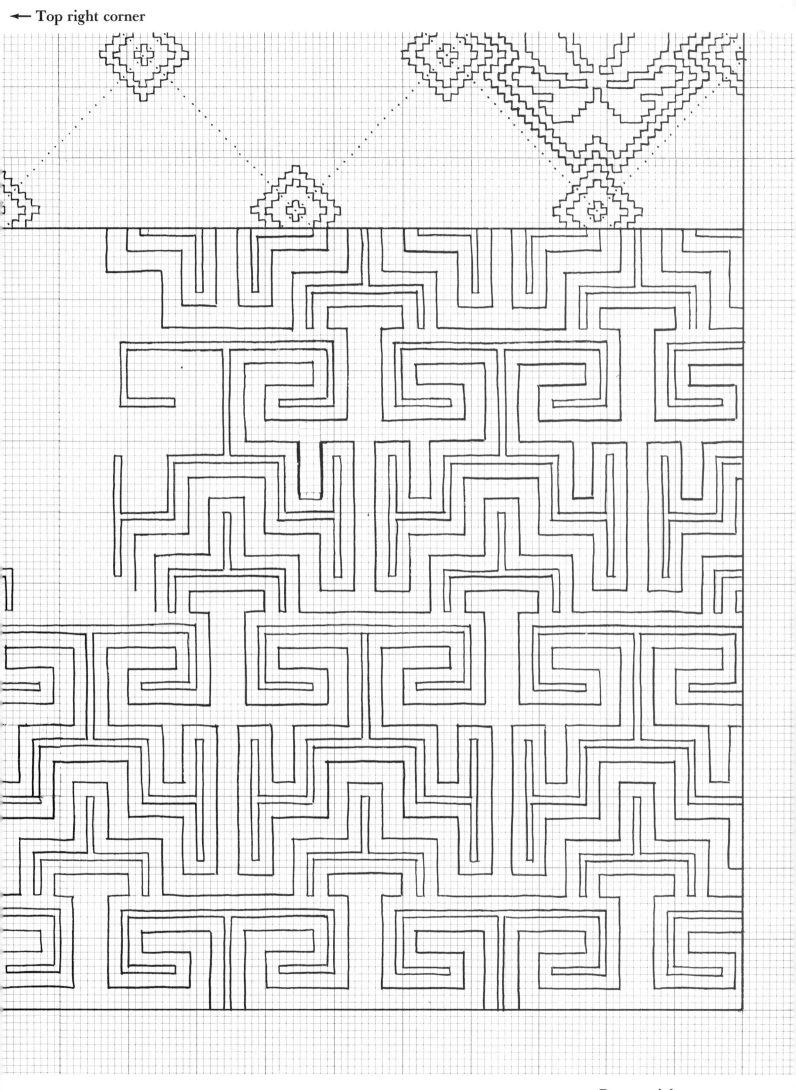

# White Kimono Panel

**The finished size is 34″ x 27″.**
**The original panel was worked on #12 canvas.**
**The graph box-stitch or thread count is 404 x 334.**

Buy a piece of #12 canvas measuring 34″ x 40″. Bind your canvas.

To duplicate the original panel, use the following colors for the cat and the kimono:

#646 medium gray D.M.C. 6-strand cotton embroidery floss
#648 light gray D.M.C. cotton
#712 off-white D.M.C. cotton
#829 cognac D.M.C. cotton
#844 dark gray D.M.C. cotton
#926 blue D.M.C. cotton
#950 pink D.M.C. cotton
#3053 green D.M.C. cotton (to touch up the cat's eyes—with non-needlepoint stitches—in order to make them as catlike as possible)

Follow the placement of colors as shown in Plate 10.

Some helpful information:

1. The three silver-gray circles across the top of the kimono (where you can put your initials and the date) are worked in basketweave with 6 strands of #648 light gray D.M.C. cotton

plus 4 strands of D.M.C. Article 281 silver filament. All 10 strands are used together in the needle. The lettering is worked in #712 off-white D.M.C. cotton.

2. The background of the kimono is worked in the brick stitch using #712 off-white D.M.C. cotton.

For the basketweave stitch on #12 canvas, use 9 strands of the D.M.C. 6-strand cotton embroidery floss. For the brick stitch on #12 canvas, use 12 strands of floss by doubling the 6 strands that cling together as you unwind the skein.

For the background, use #3013 greenish gold D.M.C. cotton and D.M.C. Article 280 gold filament.

The background of the panel is worked in the basketweave stitch, with 6 strands of #3013 plus 4 strands of gold filament. All 10 strands are used together in the needle. Each rectangle of gold leaf measures 29 stitches by 39 stitches. The gridwork—the horizontal and vertical rows separating square from square—is worked in 9 strands of #3013 D.M.C. cotton floss without the addition of the gold filaments.

For the narrow frame around the panel, use #844 dark gray D.M.C. cotton.

The design was adapted from a Japanese robe in *Period Kosode on Folding Screens*. Shojurō Nomura. Tokyo, 1940.

The original panel was worked by Maggie Lane.

Approximate time required for work: 230 hours.

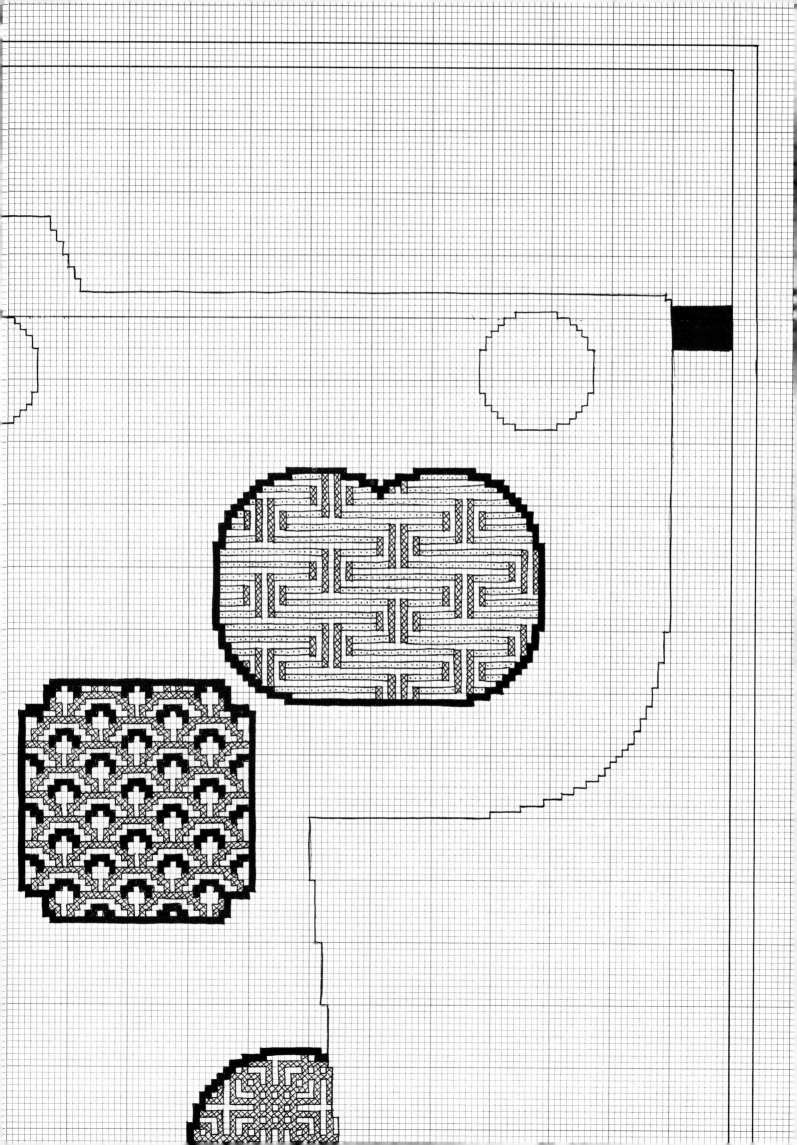

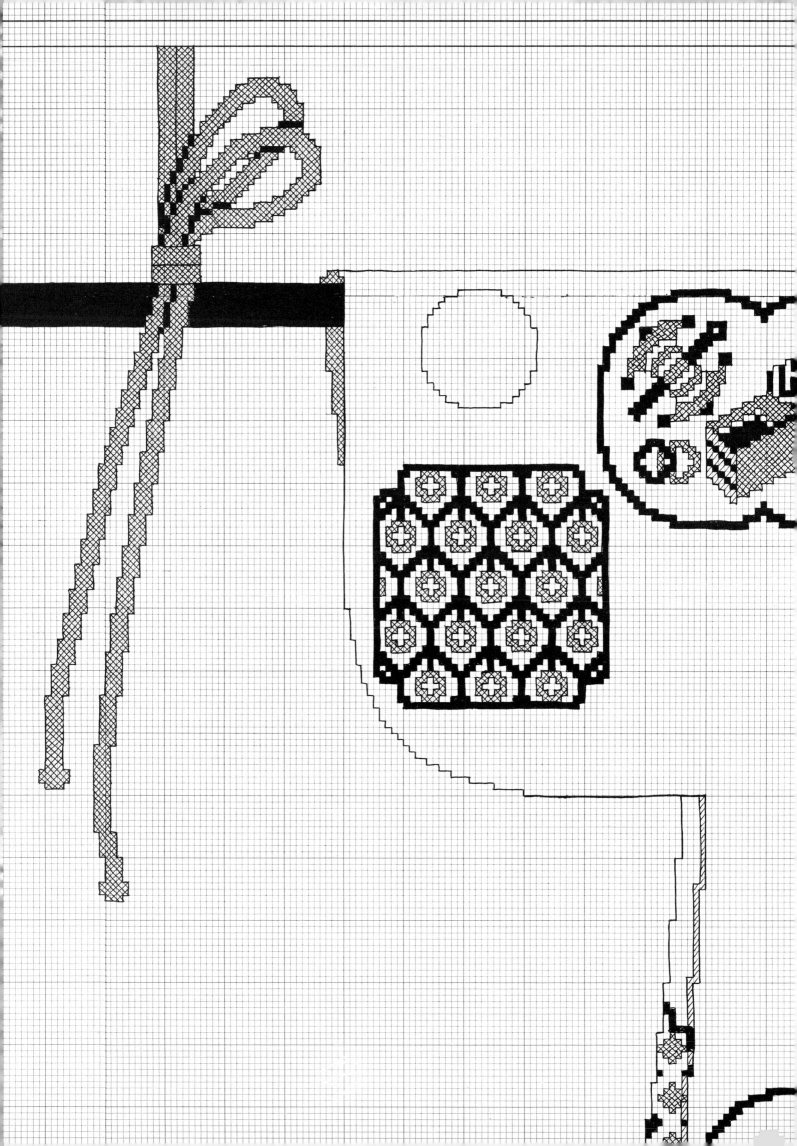

Detail of center

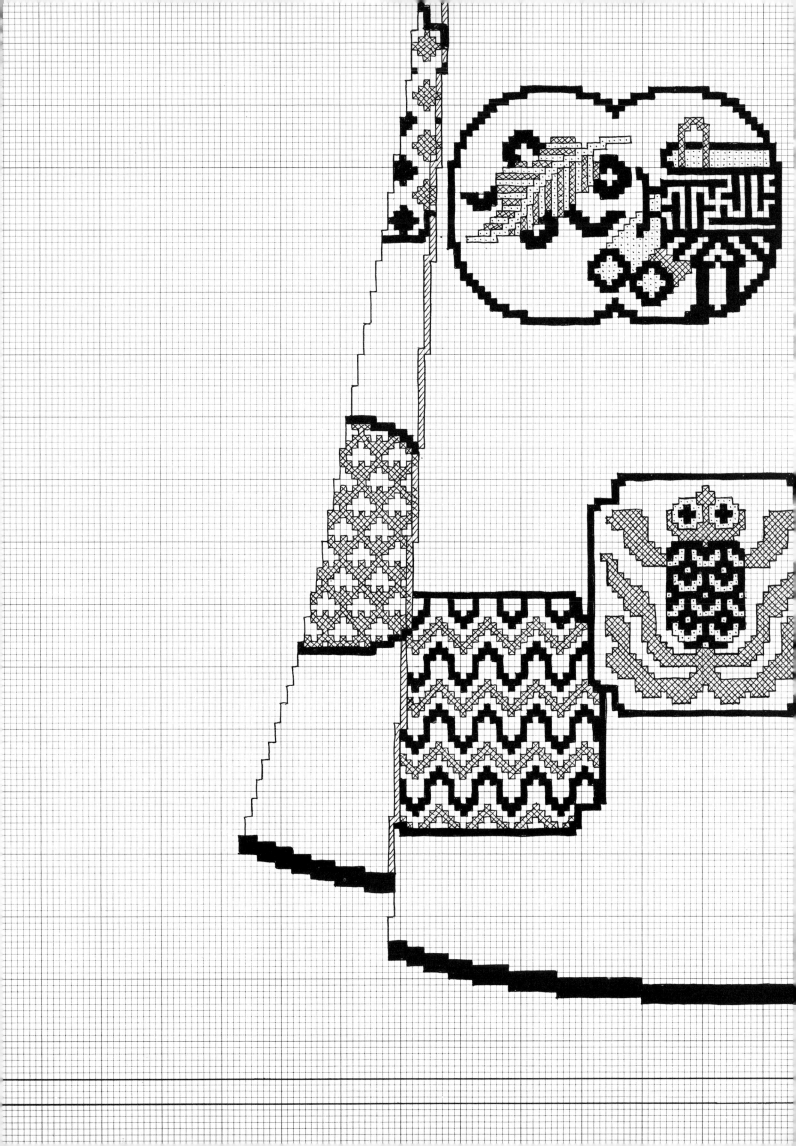

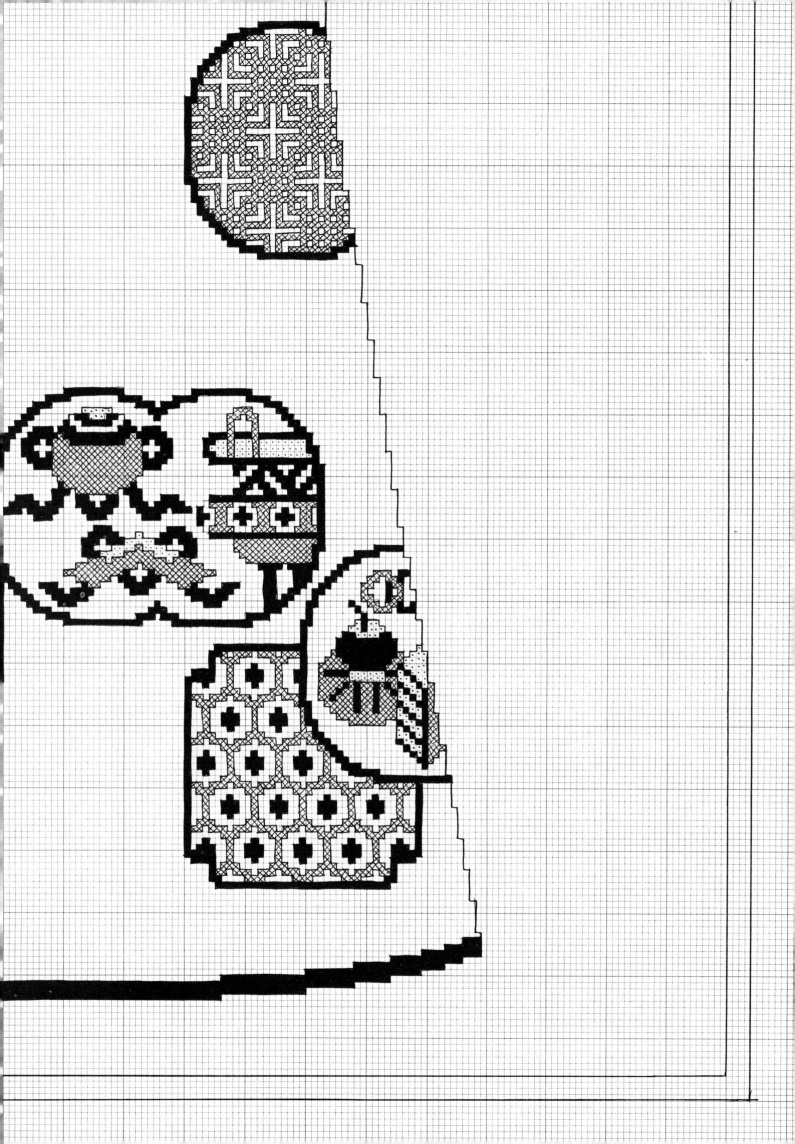

← Upper left corner

Lower left corner

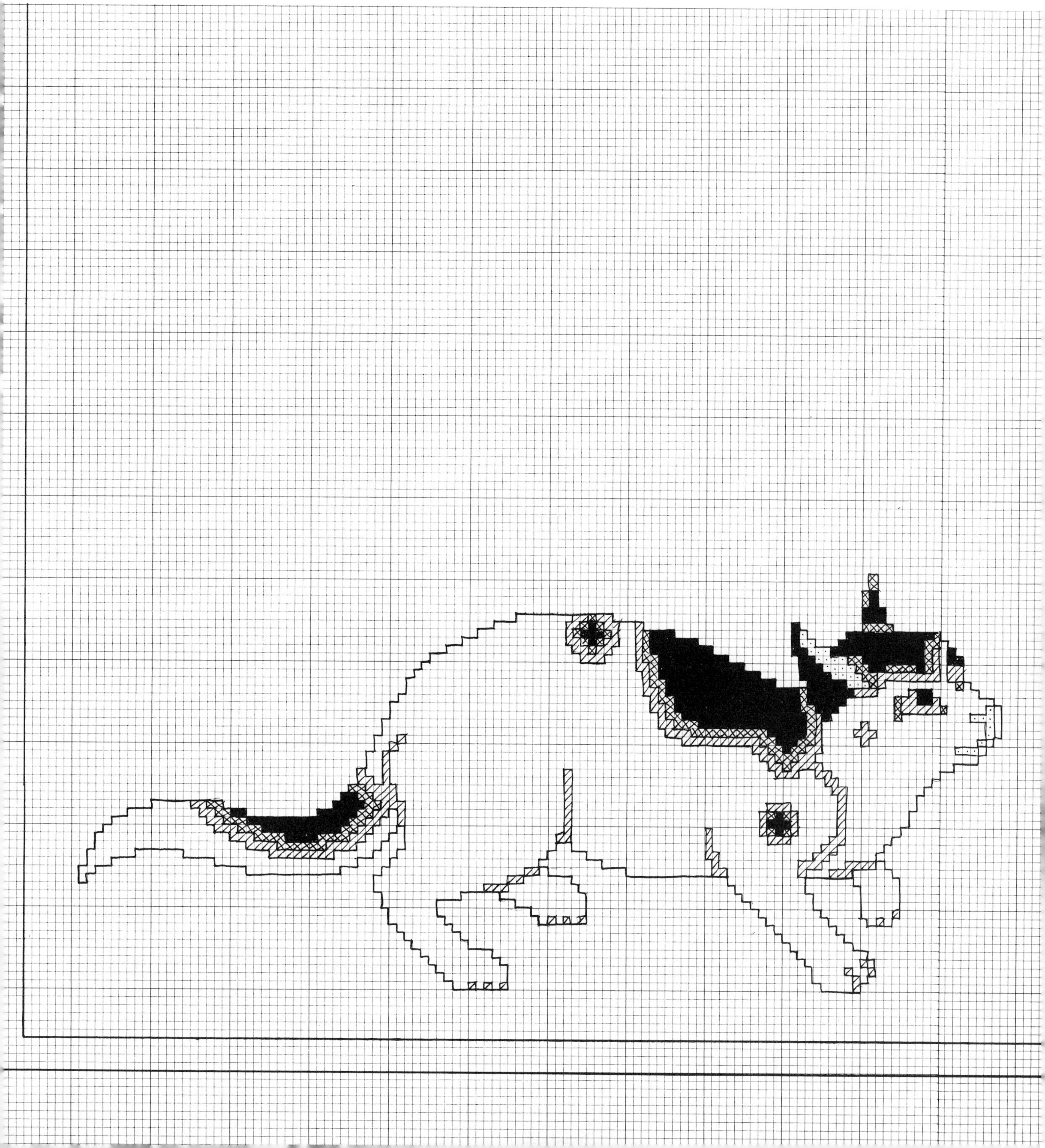

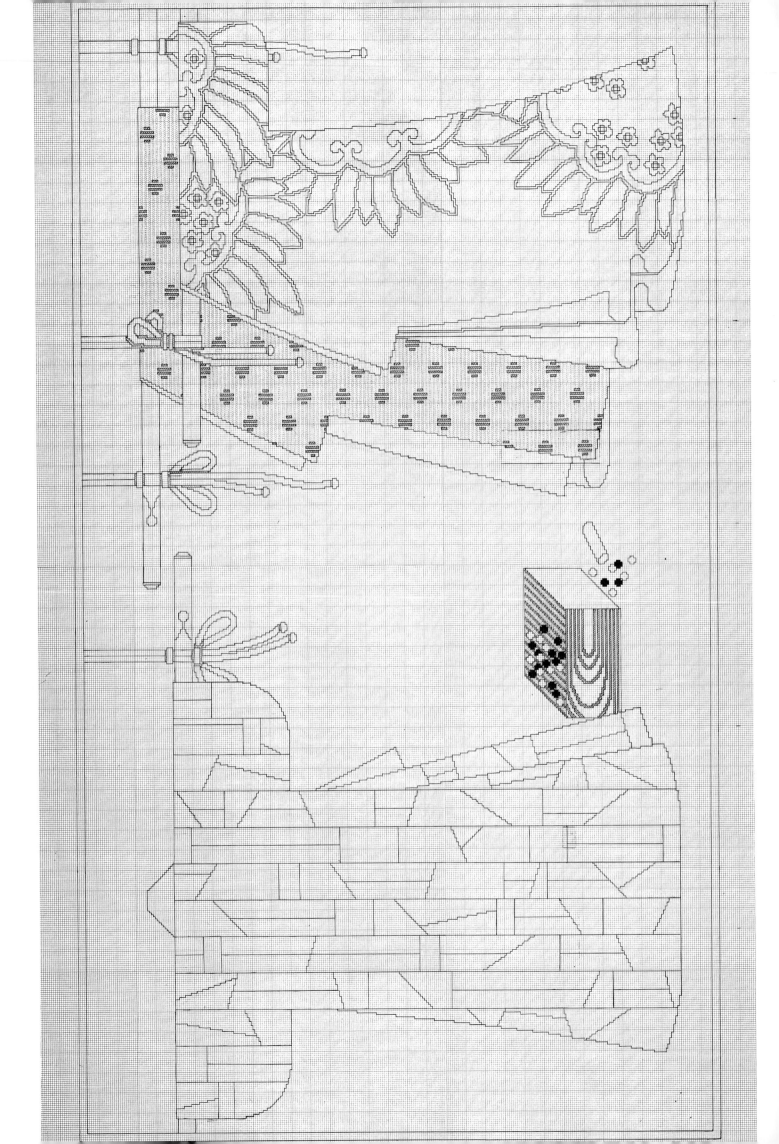

# *Three Kimonos Panel*

**The finished size is 49″ x 30″.**
**The original panel was worked on #12 canvas.**
**The graph box-stitch or thread count is 560 x 330.**

Buy a piece of #12 canvas measuring 55″ x 36″. Bind your canvas.

To duplicate the original panel, use the following colors: For the dark kimono—

#3371 dark brown D.M.C. 6-strand cotton embroidery floss (The main body of the kimono is worked in flat satin stitch, vertical rows with one slanting up to the right, one to the left, repeated to make a sort of herringbone stitch.)

#831 ginger D.M.C. cotton for small flowers with white centers

#613 khaki D.M.C. cotton for scrolls and large petals (The petals are worked in the Smyrna cross-stitch. See page 143 for diagram.)

#3064 salmon pink D.M.C. cotton for the lining of the kimono

#407 dark salmon pink D.M.C. cotton for the dark line in the lining

For the pale kimono—

#3072 ice-gray D.M.C. cotton for the horizontal lines, alternating with #712 ivory D.M.C. cotton worked in the continental stitch, but one color is done slanting in one direction (///) while the other is done slanting in the other direction (\\\), thus avoiding distortion of the canvas

    #648 gray D.M.C. cotton, all 6 strands plus 4 strands of D.M.C. Article 281 silver filament for the vertical repeat design in the pattern

    #645 dark gray D.M.C. cotton for the lining

In addition to the graph of the patchwork kimono, a color map is provided on pages 102–103. Each of the sections in each vertical row has a number, such as row 1, section 1. Always read from right to left, since needlepointers work in that direction. In each section the number is given for the D.M.C. colors used in that section.

The numbers of the colors used in the patchwork kimono are given here in numerical order. It is not "written" that you must use any or all of these colors in the patchwork kimono. I give them to you only to document the colors I used:

    #301 russet D.M.C. 6-strand cotton embroidery floss
    #311 dark blue
    #312 medium dark blue
    #322 medium blue
    #336 dark, dark blue
    #355 dark red
    #422 tan gold
    #435 tan
    #543 warm tan
    #613 gold tan
    #712 ecru
    #775 pale blue
    #823 black-blue
    #829 dark brown
    #926 soft green
    #928 celadon green
    #935 dark olive green
    #939 dark blue

#950 rosy tan
#3011 olive brown
#3012 medium olive brown
#3013 light olive brown
#3022 dark taupe
#3023 medium taupe
#3024 light taupe
#3032 sherry tan
#3033 warm beige
#3041 gray lavender
#3042 light gray lavender
#3046 soft gold
#3051 dark gray olive
#3052 medium gray olive
#3053 light gray olive
#3064 coppery tan
#3072 celadon gray
#3325 pale blue
#3371 dark brown

At the back of the book you will find graphs of small repeat patterns and diagrams of various stitches. You can use these as you wish in the patchwork kimono.

For the poles holding the kimonos:

#3371 dark brown D.M.C. cotton
#646 medium gray D.M.C. cotton
#648 light gray D.M.C. cotton for the lines

For the ribbons supporting the poles:

#225 pale pink D.M.C. cotton
#224 darker pink D.M.C. cotton
#646 gray D.M.C. cotton
#645 darker gray D.M.C. cotton
#778 pink D.M.C. cotton
#316 darker pink D.M.C. cotton

For the game box:

#3032 tan D.M.C. cotton for the top
#935 dark green D.M.C. cotton for the lines
#712 ivory D.M.C. cotton for the right side of the box
#610 brown D.M.C. cotton for the graining on the front of the box

For the playing pieces:

#3052 celadon gray D.M.C. cotton for the cylinder
#712 ivory D.M.C. cotton
#310 black D.M.C. cotton

For the background, use 3 strands of #833 gold D.M.C. cotton, 3 strands of #422 tan D.M.C. cotton, and 4 strands of D.M.C. Article 280 gold filament. All 10 strands are used together in the needle.

The background gold leaf is worked in rectangles measuring 29 stitches by 39 stitches. These rectangles are separated from each other by a grid of bare canvas threads, that is, threads that have no stitches covering them.

For the narrow frame, use #3371 dark brown D.M.C. cotton

The original panel was worked by Maggie Lane.

Approximate time required for work: 400 hours.

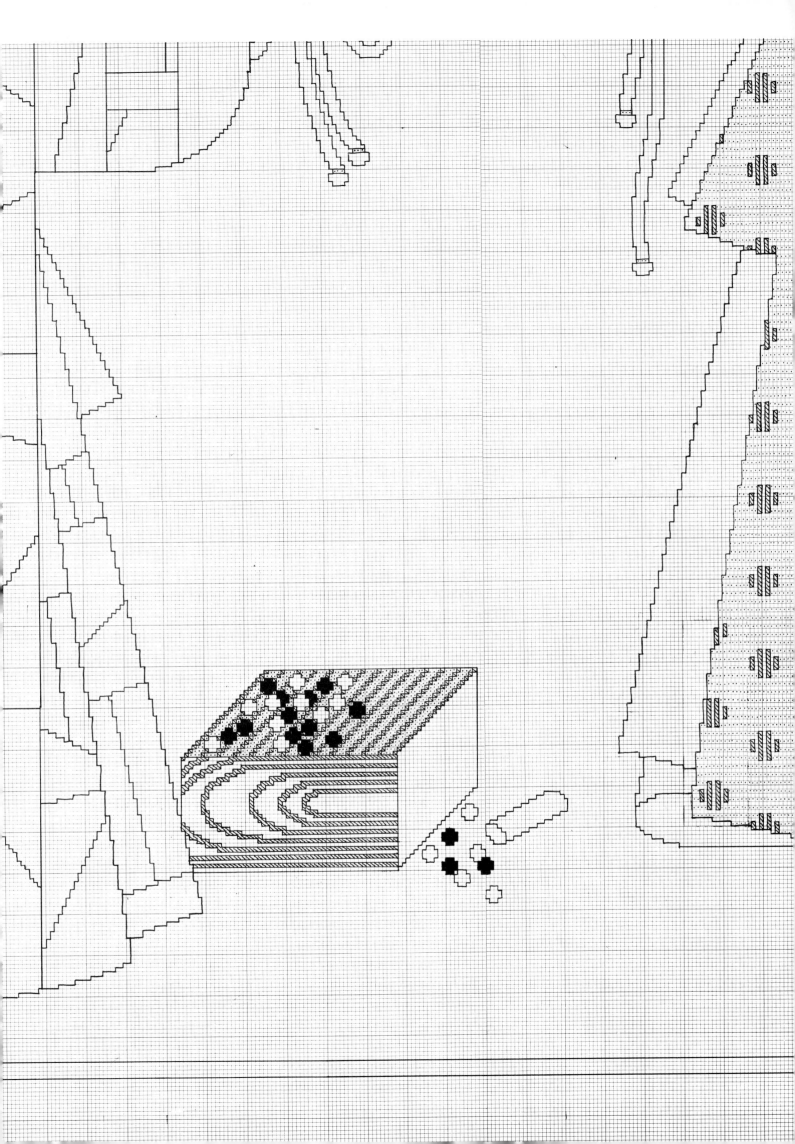

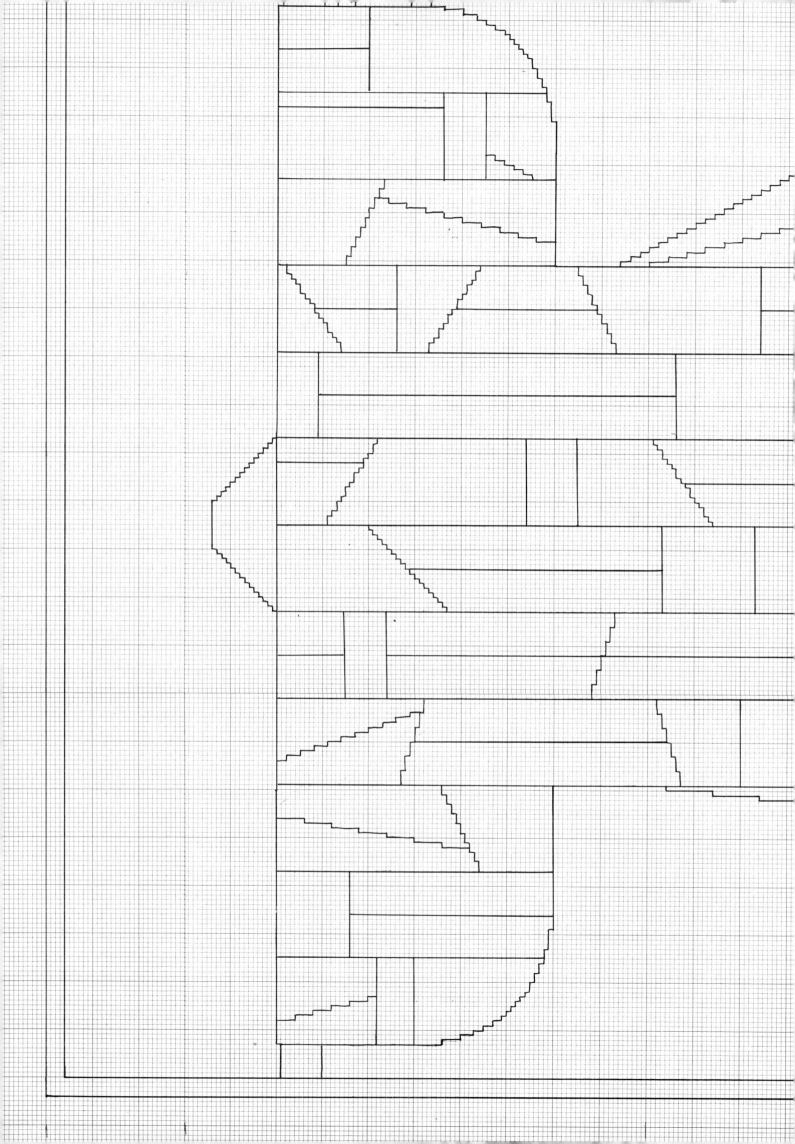

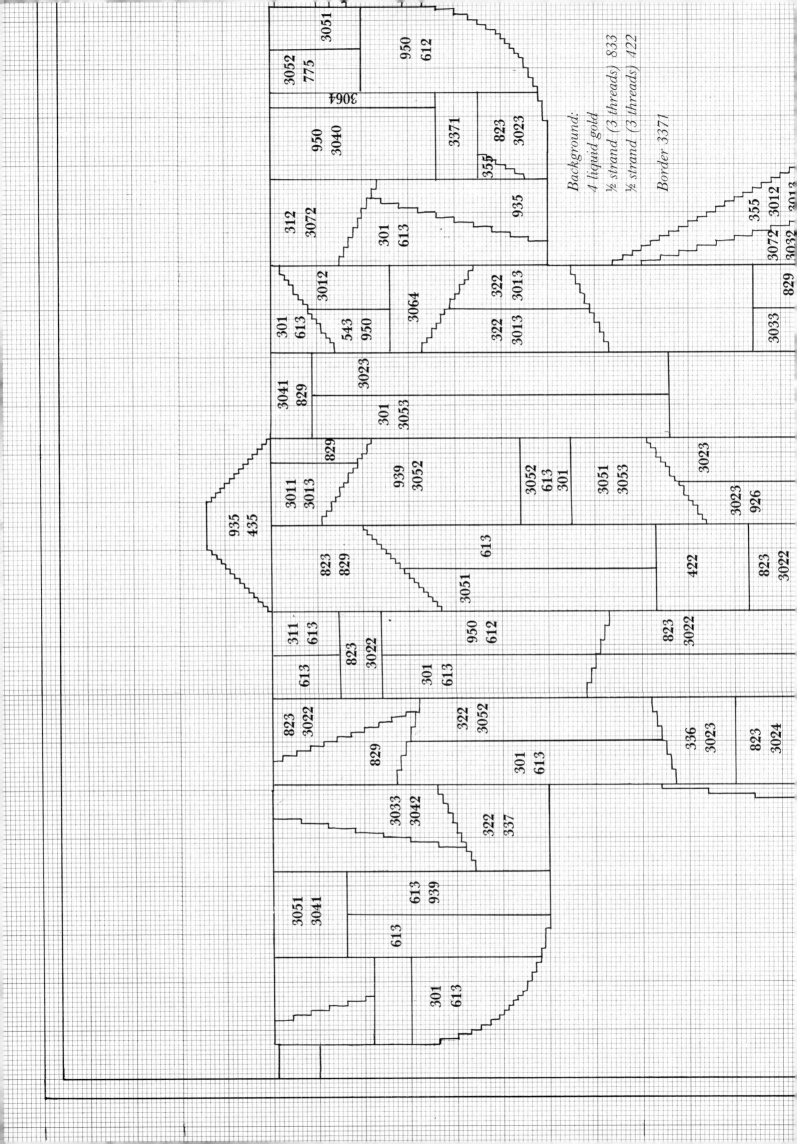

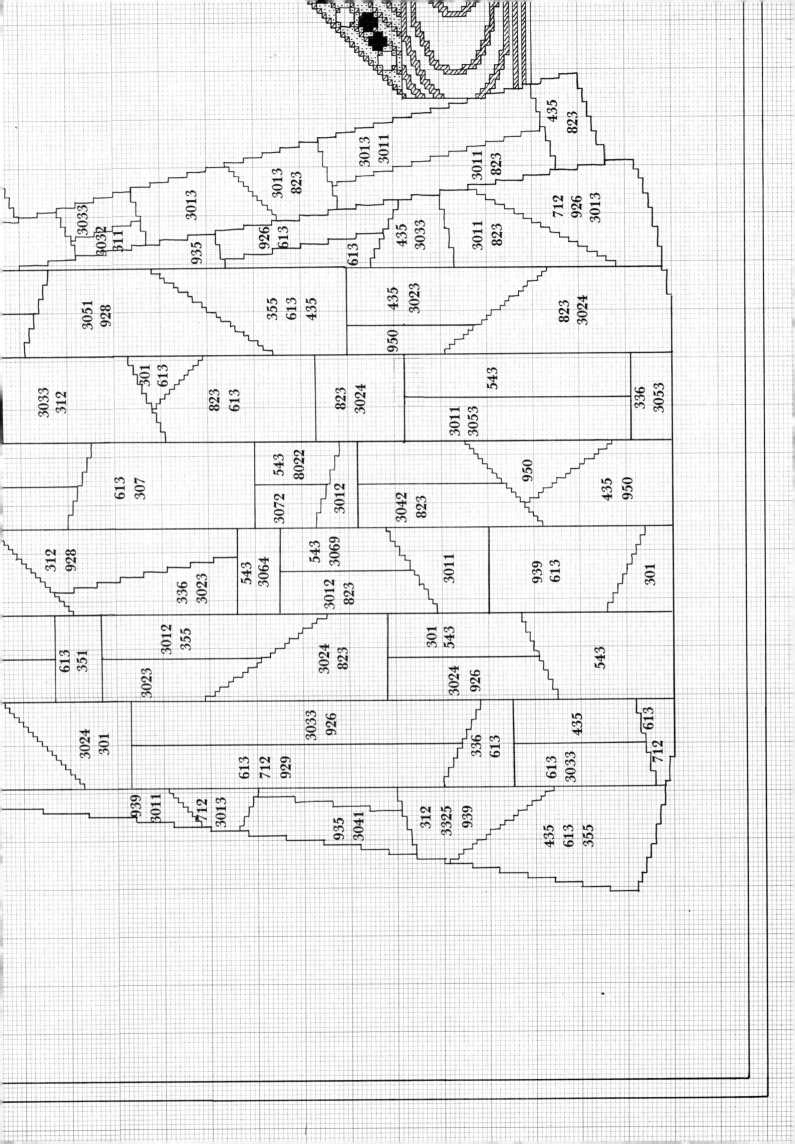

**Right side**

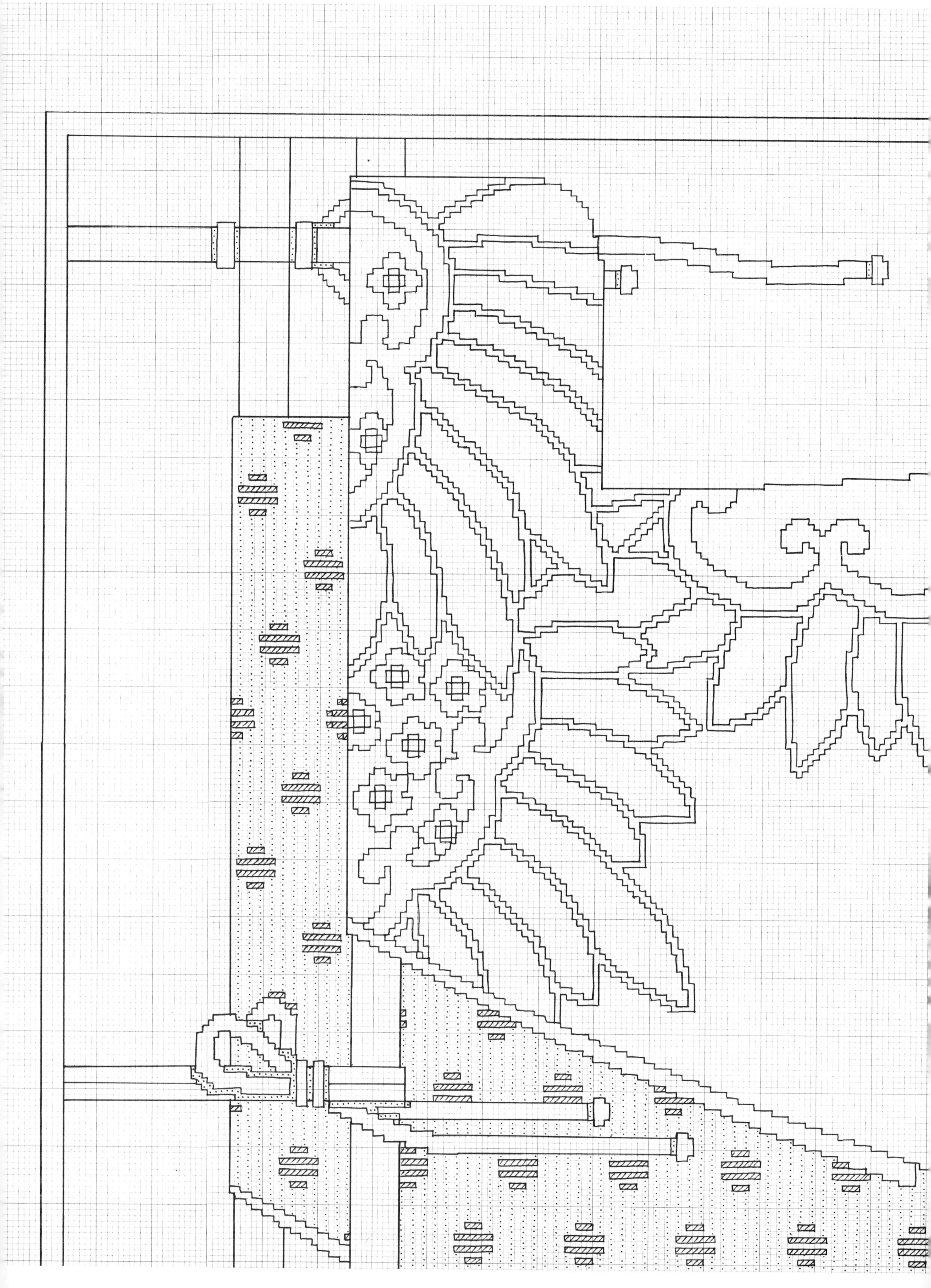

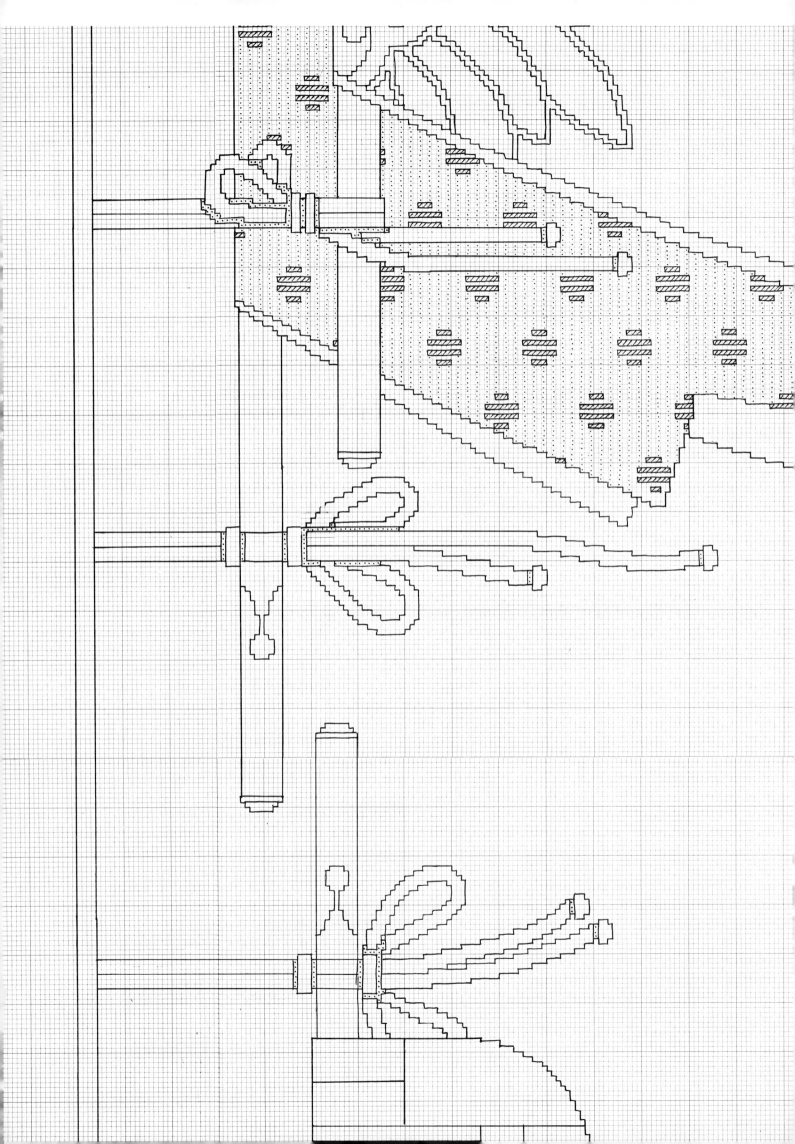

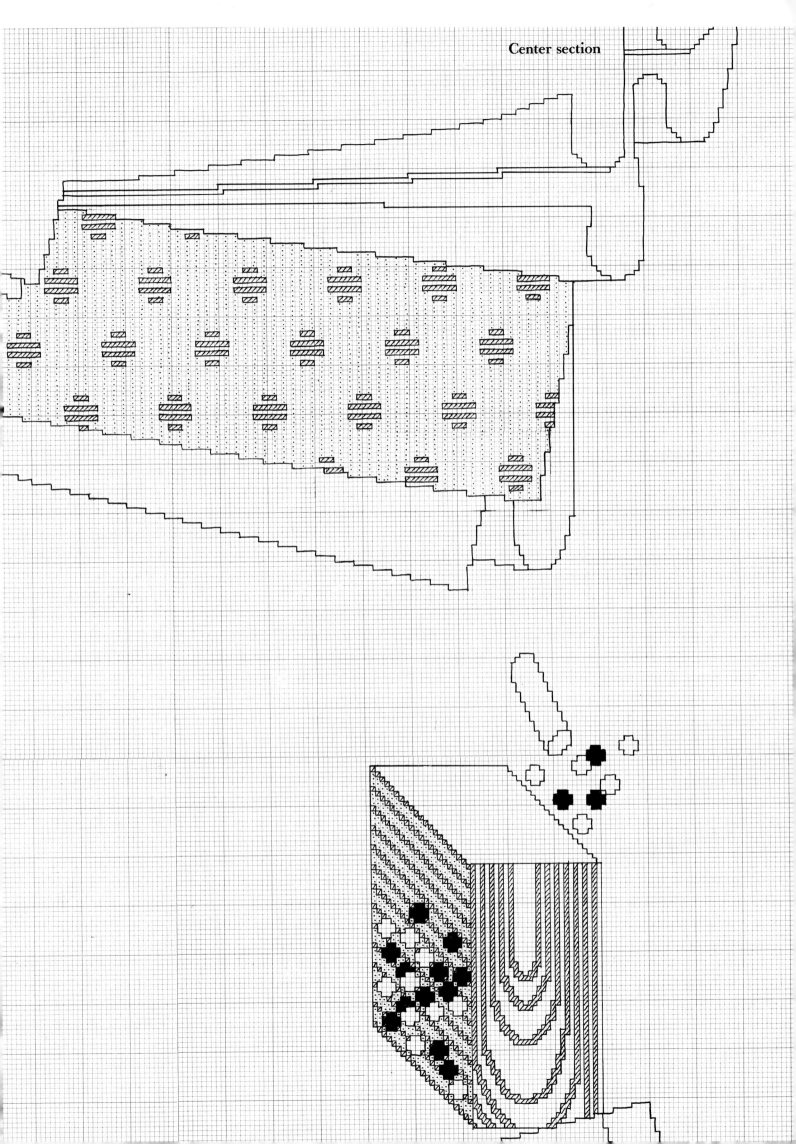

# Wagon Wheels Kimono Panel

**The finished size is 34″ x 30″.**
**The original panel was worked on #12 canvas.**
**The graph box-stitch or thread count is 404 x 330.**

Buy a piece of #12 canvas measuring 40″ x 36″. Bind your canvas.
To duplicate the original panel use the following colors:

#614 orange-red Au Ver à Soie silk
#1743 light blue silk
#1744 medium blue silk
#1745 dark blue silk
#3844 dark gray silk
#402 apricot D.M.C. 6-strand cotton embroidery floss
#613 tan D.M.C. cotton
#712 ivory D.M.C. cotton
#300 dark red D.M.C. cotton dividing the upper and lower parts of the cat-shaped box
#301 dark red D.M.C. cotton for the line on the left side of the kimono
#731 olive-green-brown D.M.C. cotton
#3022 dark taupe D.M.C. cotton for the outlines on the vertical bar of the clothing rack
Luxofil dark gold and dark silver, mixed, for the ends of the horizontal poles of the rack, the "snow-flakes" on the vertical bar of the rack, and the tiny curling waves on the kimono

With the exception of the blue waves, which are worked in the Smyrna cross-stitch (see page 143 for diagram), the entire panel is worked in the basketweave stitch.

The background of the panel is worked in rectangles measuring 29 x 39 stitches. These fill a gridwork—every thirtieth vertical row and every fortieth horizontal row—that is stitched with 6 strands of #3046 flaxen yellow D.M.C. cotton and 4 strands of D.M.C. Article 280 gold filament. All 10 strands are used together in the needle. The rectangles are stitched using the same mixture of 6 strands of #3046 and 4 strands of gold filament. The result is a kind of subliminally perceived gold leaf.

For the narrow frame around the panel, use #3844 dark gray Au Ver à Soie silk. Use all 7 strands of silk floss.

Richard Read used the following, different colors for his Kimono Panel (see Plate 13):

D.M.C. cotton #310 black
            #647 light gray
            #646 medium gray
            #645 dark gray
            #844 charcoal gray
            #3022 taupe
            #712 white cream
            #729 yellow-gold
            #680 dark yellow-gold
            #644 ecru
            #676 light yellow

D.M.C. Article 280 gold and D.M.C. Article 281 silver on the spool

Copper waves in Balger copper

The original panel (Plate 12) was worked by Maggie Lane.

Approximate time required for work: 230 hours.

Bottom left corner

**Upper right corner**

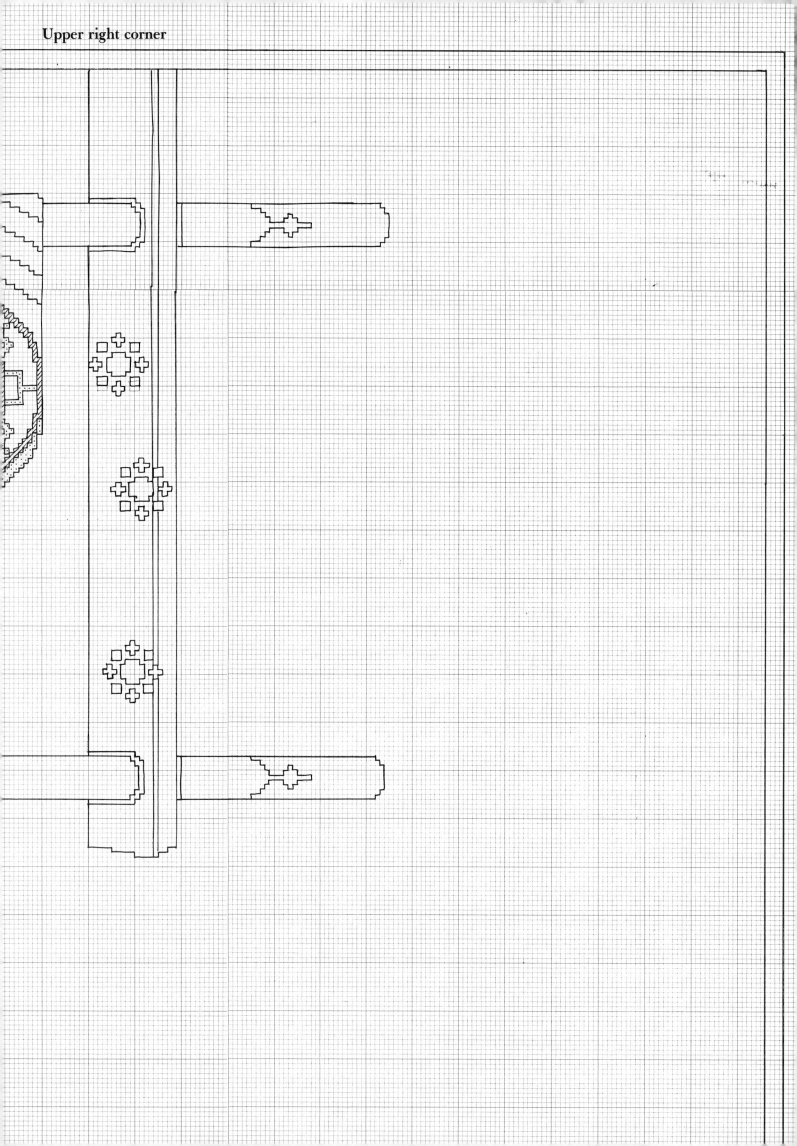

Lower right corner

# Two Horses and Groom Panel

**The finished size is 34″ x 47″.**
**The original panel was worked on #12 canvas.**
**The graph box-stitch or thread count is 410 x 570.**

Buy a piece of #12 canvas measuring 40″ x 52″. Bind your canvas.

This panel is the most advanced of all the works in the book because in it I used two colors together in the needle for almost the entire design. If the two colors are very close in tonal and chromatic value, as well as in hue, the result is appealing—a bit of visual stimulation. Cotton needlepoint can become flat looking, but two colors together in a stitch vibrate like pointillism, and simply *cannot* look dull.

This canvas was the last I worked for this book. I had so far already finished eight of the other pieces, three of the twelve having been given to friends to work. So, by the time I approached my final task, I needed something that would really excite me. The T'ang Dynasty painting of the two blooded steeds with their groom had been in my picture files for several years. In fact, I had already begun a graph of the design some time ago, then put it away because I realized I had no place to hang such a large panel. But I often thought of the design, remembering the powerful dark horse in the foreground, and his ghostly companion whose presence did not reveal itself to me on my first viewing of the painting. Then suddenly I saw a lustrous orb floating above the arched neck of the prancing stallion. Surprised, I looked for the horse belonging to the eye, found her, and fell totally in love with this masterpiece.

**121**

The two noble animals, their groom, their bridles and reins, the opulent saddle, the sense of motion caught forever—everything in the work awed me. I found the graph I had already begun and went at it again, working feverishly without stopping until I had completed it.

I attacked the needlepoint work on this panel with a fervor approaching madness. I finished the rider and the two horses in three weeks. Then I slowed down—to a trot, one might say. I then worked leisurely on the gold leaf, putting in much less time per day than I did when I first began, but I still stitched (or filled in) two squares a day.

Having said all that, let me get back to your needs.

To duplicate the panel, use the following colors:

#3022 taupe D.M.C. 6-strand cotton embroidery floss for all lines in the pale horse; for lines in the groom's face, hands, and clothes; and for the horses' hoofs

#613 tan and #950 flesh tone D.M.C. cotton for the groom's skin

#844 dark gray D.M.C. cotton for the groom's eyebrows and beard

#613 tan and #644 light taupe for the light horse and for the groom's clothes

#610 black D.M.C. cotton for the groom's eyes, the outlines of the dark horse, his saddle blanket, the groom's belt, the whisk handle, and for the reins and bridles of both horses

#844 gray D.M.C. cotton and #3836 gray Au Ver à Soie silk for the dark horse's body

#3835 gray Au Ver à Soie silk and #310 black D.M.C. cotton for the dark horse's mane and tail

For the patterned saddle:

#613 tan D.M.C. cotton
#2625 red Au Ver à Soie silk
#1434 blue Au Ver à Soie silk
#4525 light red Au Ver à Soie silk for the back of the saddle and around the #2625 red silk tassel hanging from the dark horse's bridle

The background is worked in squares measuring 40 stitches by 40 stitches, with neither an empty row nor a row of stitching separating square from square. In these squares I used several shades of gold-colored D.M.C. cotton floss. From square to square I varied the colors slightly, usually using a mixture of two shades of gold-colored cotton, though often using only one shade, but always adding 4 strands of D.M.C. Article 280 gold filament.

The following colors can be used for this kind of gold leaf:

#422 warm tan D.M.C. cotton
#613 tan D.M.C. cotton
#725 marigold D.M.C. cotton
#833 gold D.M.C. cotton
#3046 flaxen yellow D.M.C. cotton

The entire panel is worked in the basketweave stitch.

The design was adapted from a T'ang Dynasty painting by Han Kan, circa A.D. 750.

The original panel was worked by Maggie Lane.

Approximate time required for work: 400 hours.

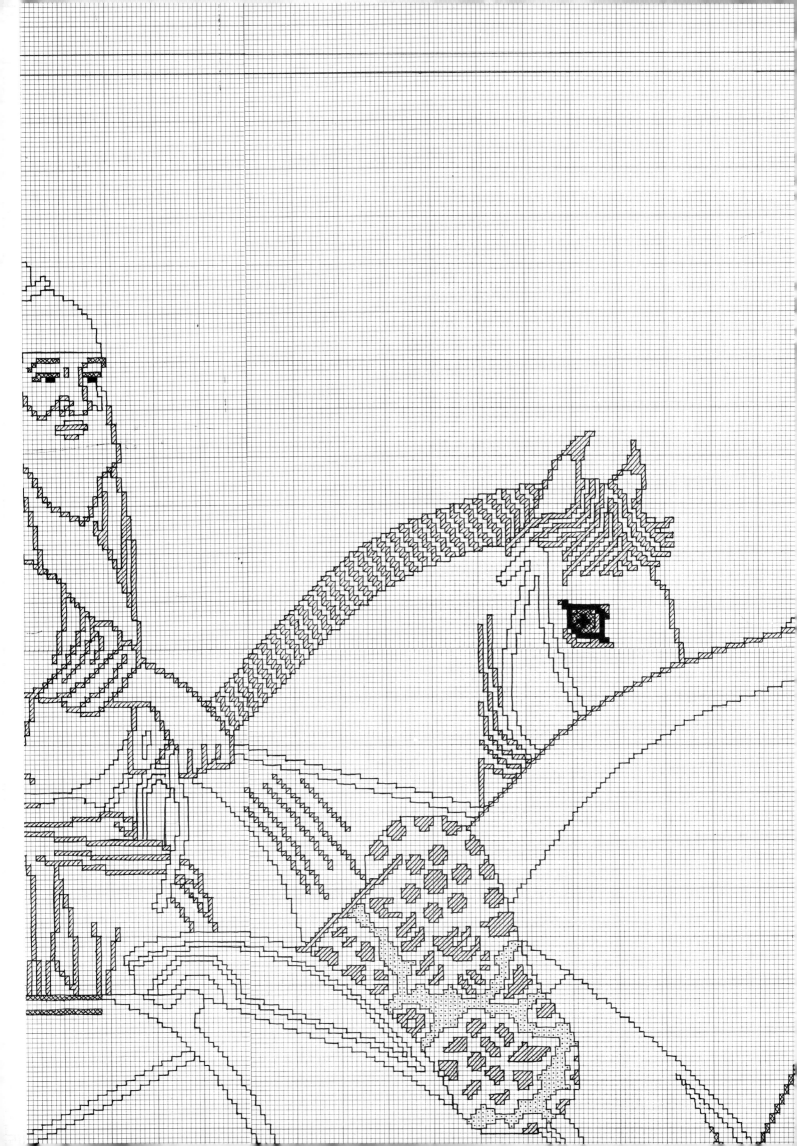

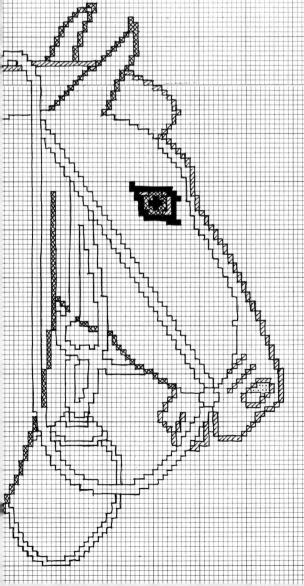

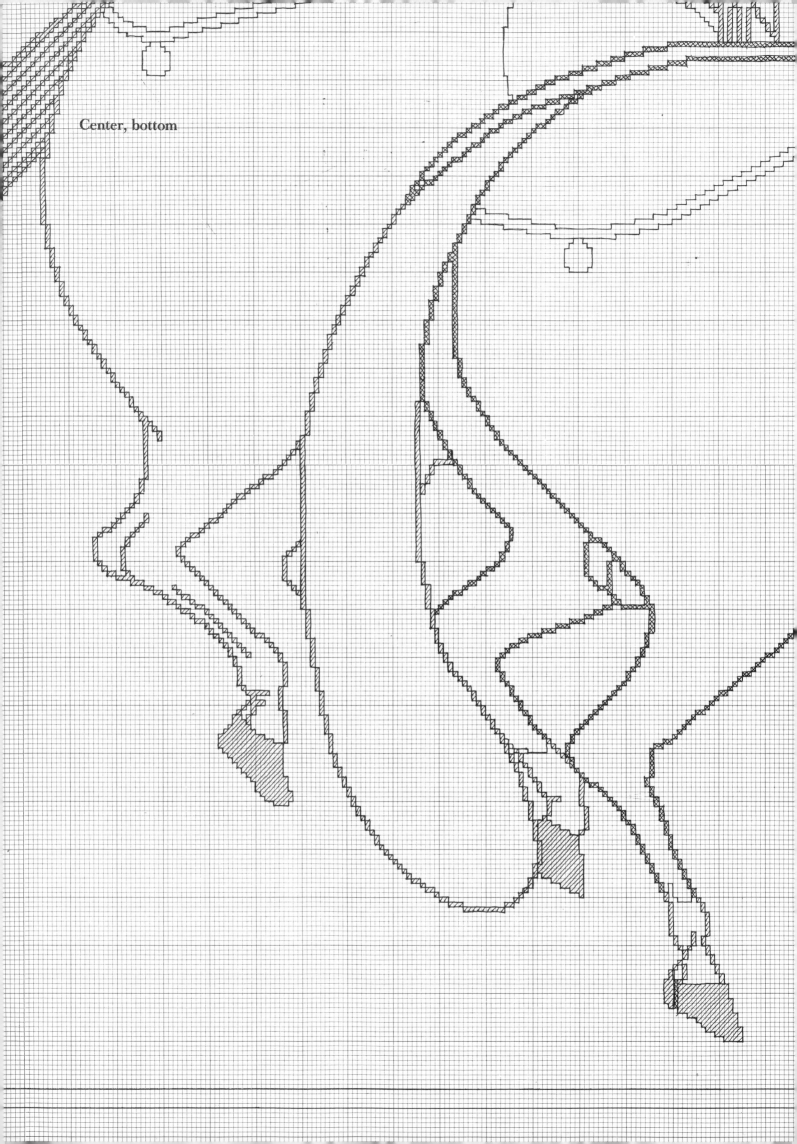

Center, bottom

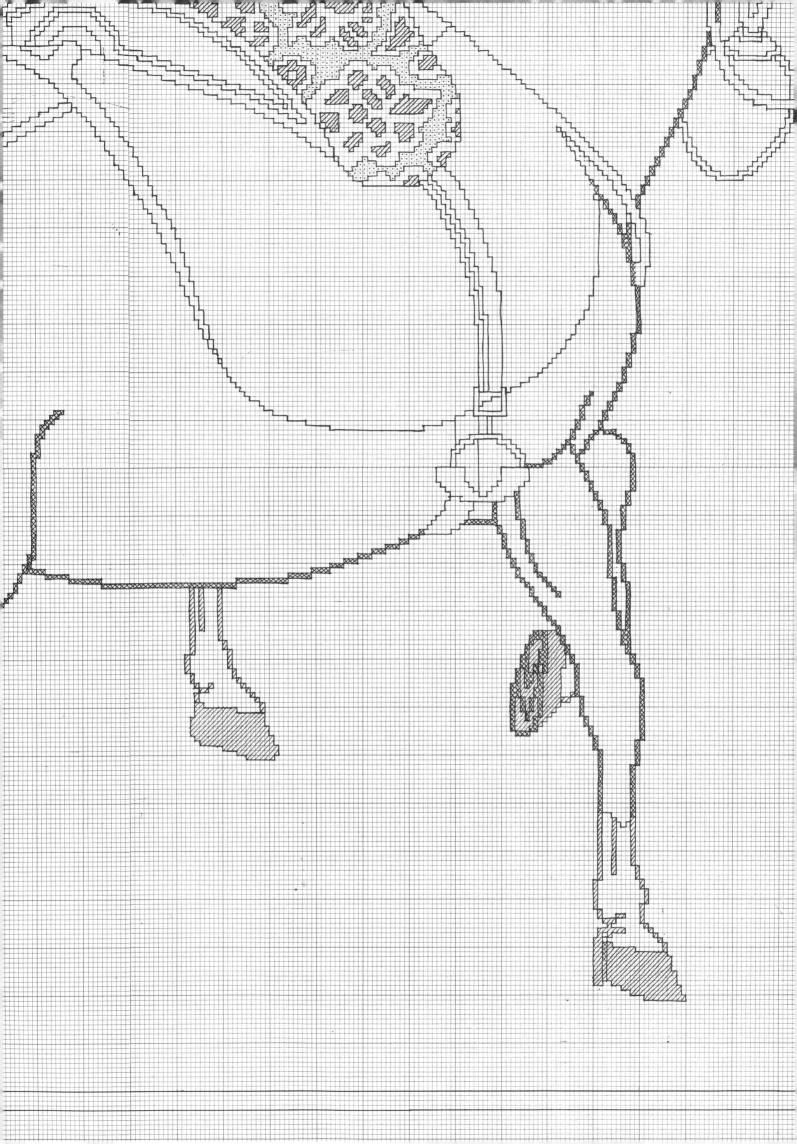

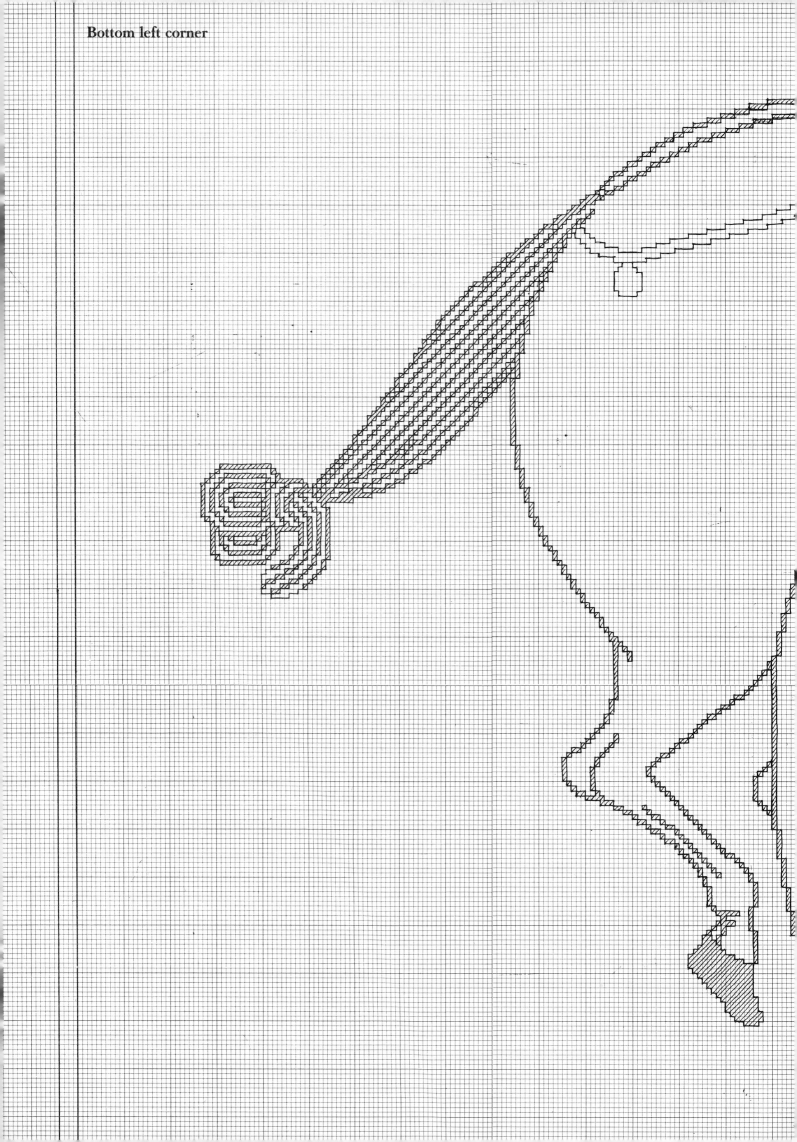

Bottom left corner

# Repeat Patterns
# and Background Designs

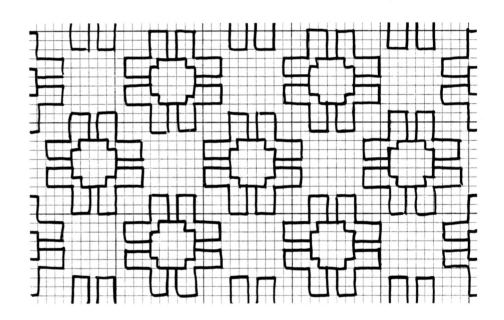

132

133

134

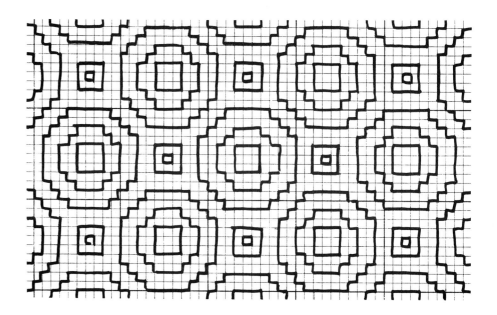

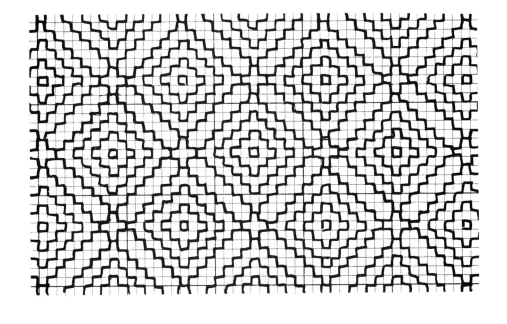

135

136

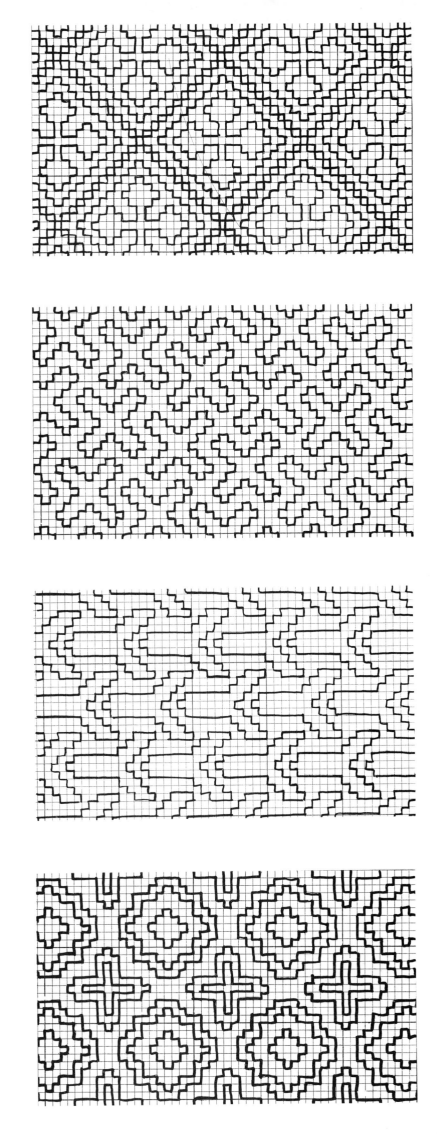

137

138

140

# The
# Stitches

# *The Stitches*

## BASKETWEAVE STITCH
Work in diagonal rows, as numbered in the diagram.

## CONTINENTAL STITCH
For single-row outlining ONLY. If this stitch is used as a background stitch, it distorts the canvas severely.

**BRICK STITCH**

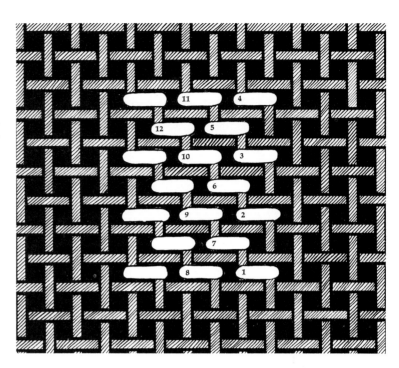

**SMYRNA CROSS-STITCH**
Work in horizontal or diagonal rows.

143

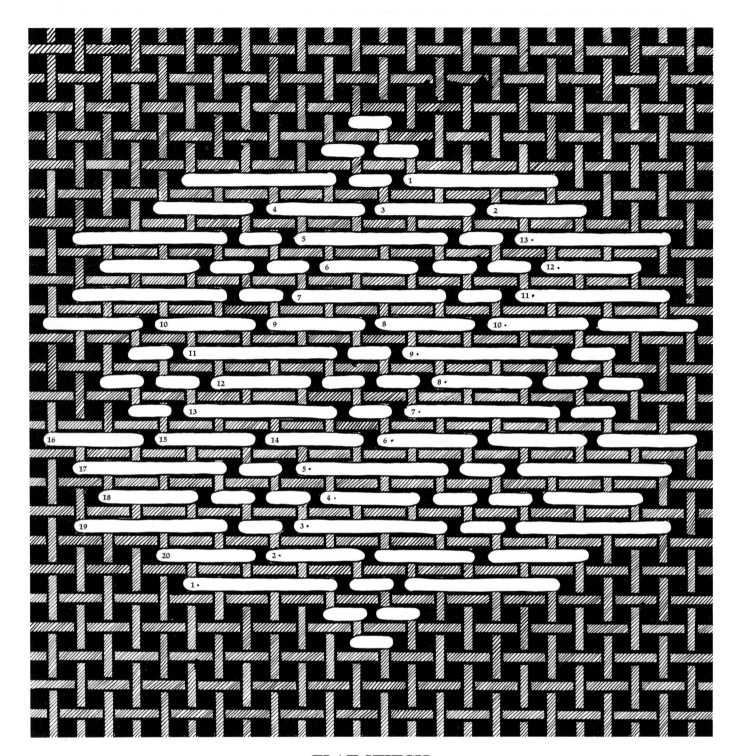

## FLAT STITCH

Medieval German whitework pattern. Work in diagonal rows. When working from the upper right to the lower left, you cover more ground than when you work from the lower left back up to the upper right. To avoid confusion, I have placed a dot after each number in the uphill sequence of stitches.

144

## BUTTONHOLE HALF MOONS

Work in diagonal rows from the lower left to the upper right, as shown in the diagram. As you can see, when you work the buttonhole stitch rather than the half eyelet shown in the first two parts of the diagram, you need a tie-down stitch, the twelfth stitch in the third, upper right-hand part of the diagram.

**IRISH STITCH**

**JACQUARD STITCH**

**LARGE CROSS-STITCH
WITH SMALL UPRIGHT CROSS
FILLER**

146

**DIAMOND CROSS-STITCH**

**CASHMERE BLOCKS**
Work in horizontal or vertical rows of blocks.

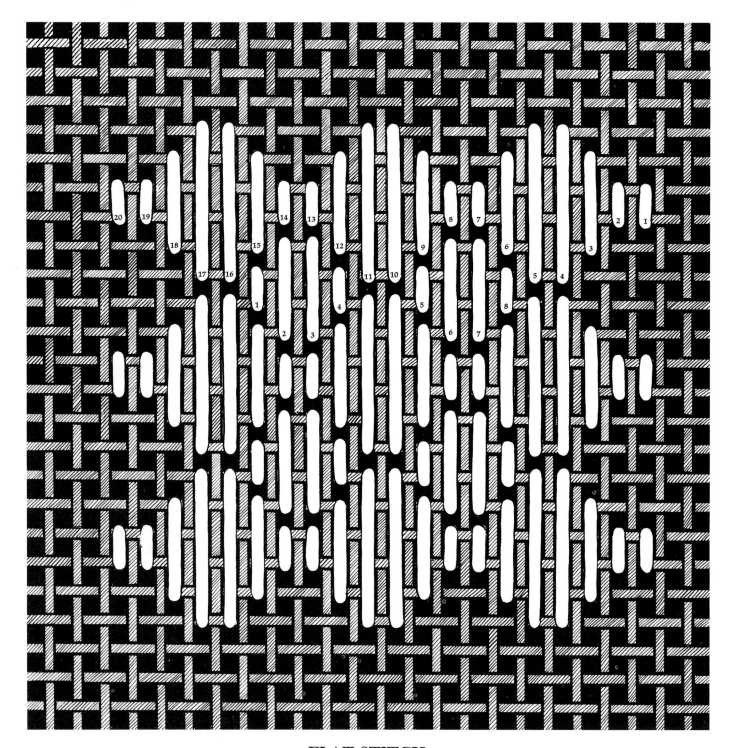

**FLAT STITCH**

148

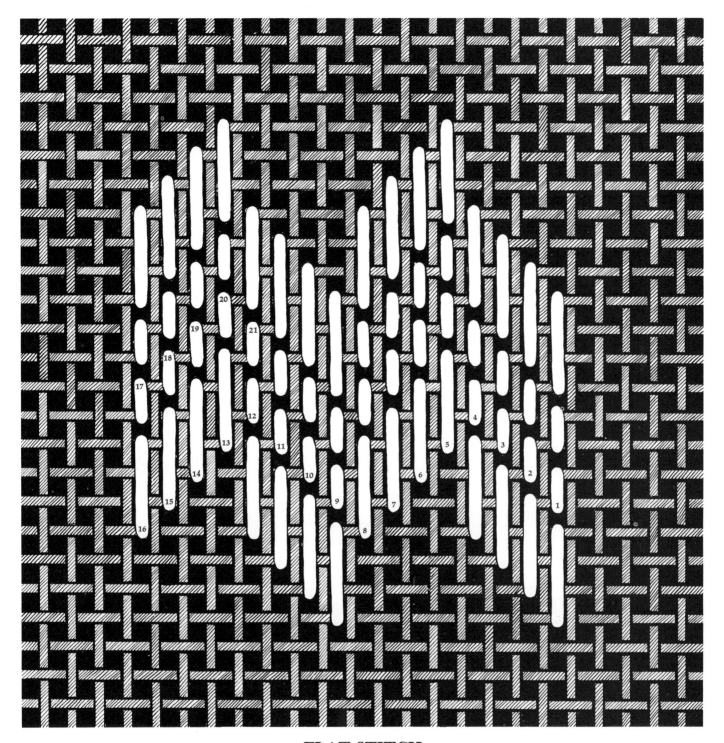

**FLAT STITCH**

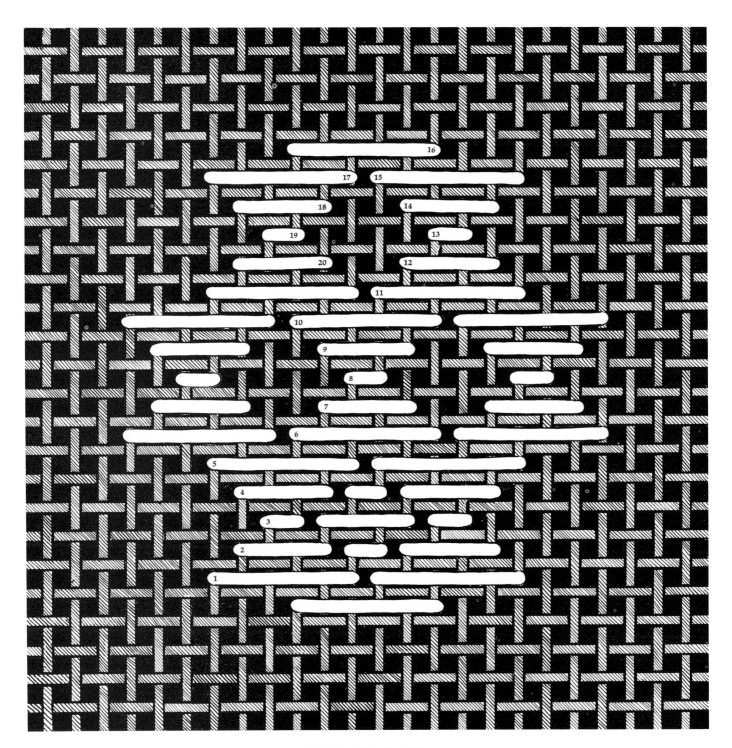

## FLAT STITCH

Work in diagonal rows. Turn canvas at end of each row so you are always working uphill to the right. Fill remaining empty diamonds with flat stitch—over two, over four, over two—as shown at the bottom of the diagram.

150

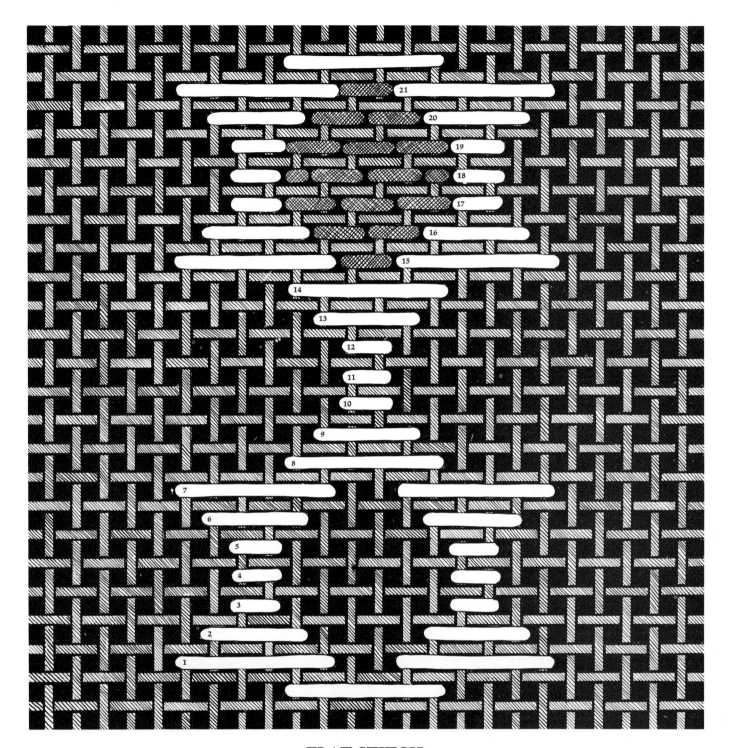

**FLAT STITCH**
Variation of a fifteenth-century German embroidery pattern.

**FLAT STITCH WITH UPRIGHT CROSS FILLER**

Work in horizontal or vertical rows of flat stitches. Work upright crosses
after all flat stitching has been completed.

152

**FLAT STITCH
WITH DIAMOND CROSS FILLER**

**FLAT STITCH
WITH SMYRNA CROSS FILLER**

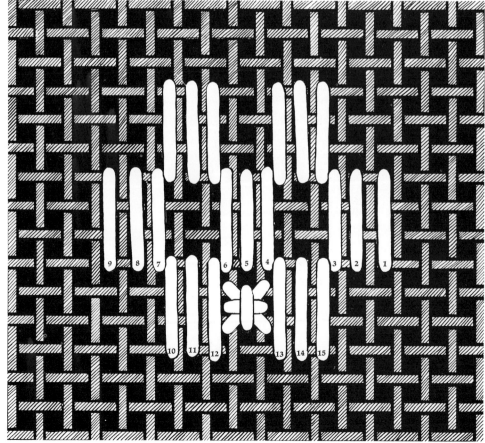

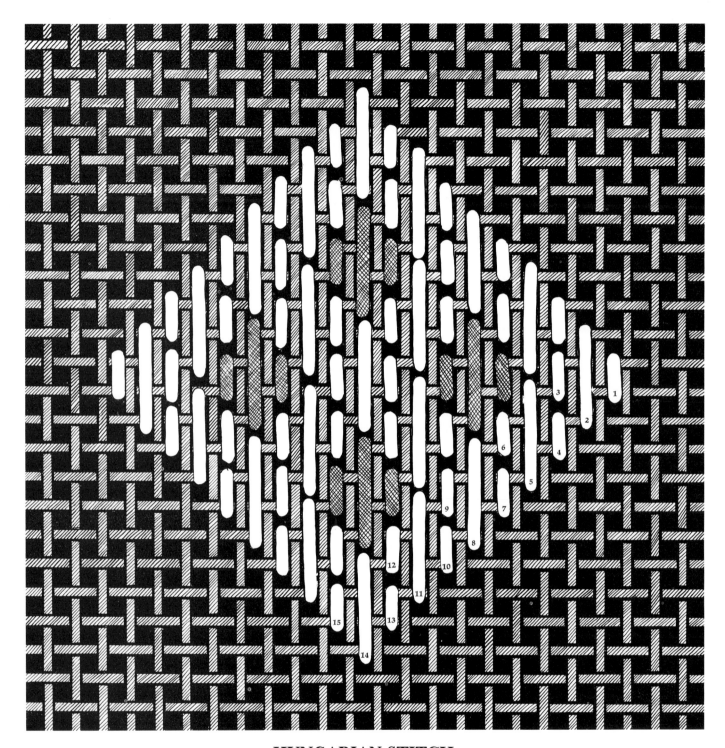

**HUNGARIAN STITCH**
Worked in two colors to create a tonal pattern.

154

# Suppliers

The retail mail-order source I recommend for all canvases and materials listed in this book is:

Margot Gallery, Inc.
26 West 54th Street
New York, New York 10019

For custom-made needlepoint handbags I recommend:

Artbag Creations, Inc.
735 Madison Avenue, at 64th Street
New York, New York 10021

# Bibliography

*Art Deco.* Victor Arwas. New York: Harry N. Abrams, Inc., 1980.

*Chinese Pictorial Art as Viewed by the Connoisseur.* R. H. Van Gulik. Rome: Instituto Italiano per il Medio ed Estremo Oriente, 1958.

*Chinese Rugs Designed for Needlepoint.* Maggie Lane. New York: Charles Scribner's Sons, 1975.

*Genre Screens from the Suntory Museum of Art.* Okada Jō. New York: Japan Society, 1978.

*Masterpieces of Chinese Album Painting in the National Palace Museum.* Taipei, Taiwan: National Palace Museum, 1971.

*A Pageant of Pattern for Needlepoint Canvas.* Sherlee Lantz and Maggie Lane. New York: Atheneum, 1973.

*Period Kosode on Folding Screens.* Shojirō Nomura. Tokyo, 1940.

*Printed Cottons of Asia.* Tamezo Osumi. Tokyo: Bijutsu Shuppansha; Rutland, Vt.: Charles E. Tuttle Co., 1963.

*Rugs and Wall Hangings.* Maggie Lane. New York: Charles Scribner's Sons, 1976.

*Textile Designs of Japan.* Osaka: Japan Textile Color Design Center, 1959.